Autism, Pedagogy and Education

Carmel Conn

Autism, Pedagogy and Education

Critical Issues for Value-based Teaching

palgrave
macmillan

Carmel Conn
School of Education, Early Years
and Social Work
University of South Wales
Newport, UK

ISBN 978-3-030-32559-6   ISBN 978-3-030-32560-2   (eBook)
https://doi.org/10.1007/978-3-030-32560-2

This Palgrave Pivot imprint is published by the registered company Springer Nature Switzerland AG
The registered company address is: Gewerbestrasse 11, 6330 Cham, Switzerland

Foreword

It would seem it is now part of the job of the contemporary academic to wade through numerous offers for their time, yet occasionally something interesting drops into one's inbox. This happened to me when I was asked to review a submission for a book. This unusually interesting submission then grew into the text you are now about to read.

In this book, Carmel Conn expertly weaves together her own research with reflections regarding educational ideology and practice in relation to autistic learners. From the outset case study examples are utilised to highlight educational practice in an informative and respectful way, showing how such activities are interactional and situational and reminding readers that interactions within educational settings are ongoing accomplishments.

With some notable exceptions, it is rare that the voices of autistic young people are listened to within research regarding their education. Carmel Conn is one of a few researchers pioneering methods through which to do just that. Traditionally, guides regarding the teaching of autistic young people have often stereotypically framed issues through a medical or behavioural model perspective. The perspective presented here asks the reader to move beyond such constraints to an inclusive pedagogy.

A theme throughout is the importance of relationships to the implementation of inclusive pedagogy, contrasted with a critique of normative remedial models of 'expert' knowledge often at odds with progressive educational philosophies as well as the voices of autistic activists and scholars. In so doing, the instrumentalist ideology of education as the transference of normative knowledge and skills is problematised. Examining the everyday interactions of practitioners and autistic learners, this book delves into what constitutes effective pedagogy. Rather than perceiving autism as a set of deficits to correct and remediate, this story is contrasted with a more progressive, respectful alternative. In this way a tension is revealed between educational and therapeutic values and cultures. As the first case study that opens the book demonstrates however, autistic learners do not progress by becoming or acting less autistic, but by being allowed to thrive in accessible environments, building a sense of belonging within a community of practice.

Carmel Conn asks numerous questions that need to be asked in relation to what constitutes a good education, exposing competing ideologies and priorities. She explores both the agency of teachers and that of young autistic learners (too often perceived as a passive recipient of intervention). Drawing upon the work of various disciplines as well as numerous autistic scholars and writers, she addresses differential embodiment and sense-making in relation to autistic people. Whilst some writers may have attempted to address some of these concerns, it is very rare to see these various aspects collated together as it has been in this book, and in making such a persuasive case for an inclusive pedagogical approach.

Carmel Conn asks the reader to see a young autistic person, not as a problem to be resolved, but to recognise their strengths, to ask how one can make an environment more accessible, suggesting bespoke support be strategically applied only when necessary and not as a general rule of an increased reliance on specialists. In terms of a future for educational practice for autistic learners, I would wholeheartedly agree. I hope that this book is read widely and that the reader will be encouraged to move beyond a purely deficit model of autism and reflect upon their own everyday interactions with autistic learners in a new way.

Canterbury, UK   Dr. Damian Milton

Acknowledgements

This book is about people's lived experiences in schools—children's and adult's—and their everyday interactions with each other. In writing about this subject, I am drawing partly on my knowledge and experience as a teacher who worked in schools for many years. I would like to thank the people I met during that time who have helped me to think more clearly about what goes on when pupils learn and how teachers support them in this.

The book is also based on my postdoctoral research and I would like to thank the pupils, teachers, parents and schools who participated in this project. The research relied on people trusting me with video recordings of their real-time interactions in classrooms and I am most grateful for the wholehearted and helpful ways in which participants joined in with the project, shared their thoughts and contributed to interpretations of the data. Without their interest, this book would not have been possible.

I would also like to thank the Masters students I have taught in recent years whose discussions have informed the arguments I set out here. Thanks go too to my colleagues Matt Hutt and Stephanie Warman who provided me with feedback on parts of the manuscript.

Anonymous reviewers on articles related to the research reported here helped to develop my thinking on the subject of education, inclusive practices and autistic pupils and I would like to acknowledge their support. Thanks to Eleanor Christie at Palgrave Macmillan for commissioning the book and to Rebecca Wyde for her editorial assistance. I would particularly like to thank Dr. Damian Milton who provided detailed feedback as the writing progressed and who has agreed to produce a foreword for the book.

Contents

Transcription Conventions

The detailed transcriptions of child-adult and teacher-pupil talk that are presented in Chapters 2 and 3 are based on conventions originally developed by Gail Jefferson (Sacks et al. 1974) and typically used in conversation analysis. Specific transcription conventions used in the book are based on those developed by Sidnell (2010) are as follows:

[	Beginning of overlap in turns
]	End of overlap in turns
=	Turn follows with no gap (latching)
(2.5)	Pause in seconds
(.)	Very short pause
:::	Elongation of vowel sound
<u>word</u>	Utterance is emphasized
°word°	Utterance is said in a softer voice
↓	Falling intonation
↑	Rising intonation
<word>	Elongated talk
>word<	Fast talk
((action))	Description of speaker actions

Reference

Sacks, H., Schegloff, E., & Jefferson, G. (1974). A simplest systematics for the organisation of turn-taking for conversation. *Language, 50*(4), 696–735.

Sidnell, J. (2010). *Conversation analysis: An introduction.* Chichester: Wiley-Blackwell.

1

Introduction: A Teacher and a Pupil Interact

Abstract The introductory chapter provides an extended vignette of one autistic child, Maab, aged five, and her experience of school. It is described how her interactions with her teacher create a learning environment that supports an increasing sense of safety at school and growing confidence as a learner, but also change and development within her teacher. The focus of the book is explained, namely what supports good education for autistic pupils, with the argument made that this does not necessarily concern the wider dissemination of specialised practices and specialist knowledge to mainstream or general education settings. The issue of teachers' beliefs about the purpose of education is raised and the notion of value-based teaching is introduced with reference to current conceptualisations of inclusive pedagogy.

Keywords Education for autistic pupils · Purpose of education · Value-based teaching

© The Author(s) 2019
C. Conn, *Autism, Pedagogy and Education*,
https://doi.org/10.1007/978-3-030-32560-2_1

1

Maab, aged five-years-old, sometimes cries as she comes through the school gates in the mornings. She finds the experience of going to her mainstream school an overwhelming one, but her mother, Maryam, finds it hard to understand exactly why. Mrs James, Maab's teacher, doesn't understand either and feels rather helpless about the situation. She is usually able to form good relationships with the children in her class, but Maab doesn't seem to respond well to her friendly approach. Mrs James had an autistic pupil in her class once before. She remembered at the time being told to introduce a quiet activity at the start of the day since this child had also found it hard to make the transition from home to school. Mrs James knows that Maab likes to draw so she sets up a small table in one corner of the classroom where she knows Maab will not be disturbed. Each morning she or her classroom assistant meet Maab with her mother and invite her to sit at the table to draw. Maab loves to draw and feels much happier when she can sit quietly doing this for a while, undisturbed by anyone during that time.

As a teacher, Mrs James believes firmly that children are capable as learners, though she knows from experience that some need support to be able to make progress. Mrs James believes strongly in supporting children and doing her best for all the children in her class. She believes that taking an interest in children as individuals is really important. She often asks children about their ideas and pastimes and takes very seriously any concerns they bring to her. Mrs James can see that drawing is something that is important to Maab. Maab likes to draw little characters that look like rabbits. Her drawings are very inventive and often depict the homes, shops and playgrounds of these creatures. Mrs James is curious about them and asks Maab to explain, listening attentively to what she has to say.

Mrs James tries hard to think about Maab's experience of her class-room. She takes time to observe Maab as she goes about different learning activities and tries to imagine what Maab's experience might be. She often talks to other people who know Maab well, including Maryam, Maab's mother, and Mrs Williams who taught Maab when she was in Reception class. Mrs James also talks to the teaching assistant, Lucy Bassett, who supports Maab for literacy and numeracy lessons in the mornings and to Nicola James, the teacher who co-ordinates extra support for children. Everyone realises that something is upsetting Maab during lesson-time, but they are not exactly sure what it is. Mrs James wonders if it might be the digital timer she puts up on the whiteboard to tell children how much time they have left to finish their task. The timer is a large animated cartoon of a globe-shaped bomb with a slow-burning fuse that eventually explodes. Maab finds that the animation makes her feel panicked and doesn't know what to do about it. She puts her fingers in her ears and tries to look away when the animation is put up on the whiteboard. Mrs James notices this and decides that she is going to stop using this timer. Though some of the children in her class enjoy it, Mrs James finds another animation that everyone likes and uses this instead.

Mrs James believes that as a teacher it is very important for her to find out about how children in her class are making sense of learning and about any questions they have. This, she believes, allows her to support them in moving forward in their thinking. Mrs James likes to talk to children and ask them what they think about something. She always encourages them to explain some aspect of their learning and say more about their ideas. Some children in her class are weaker in their ability to express themselves, but Mrs James does not see this as a barrier to their participation in talk about their learning. She tries to be open and respectful in her communication with her pupils, building relationships where children feel they are listened to. Mrs James believes it is important to try to tune into the different ways that children communicate. For example, with Maab, she notices that just listening to her and not interrupting too much is a good way of interacting.

As the academic year progresses, Mrs James notices that Maab seems more settled in school. Maryam, Maab's mother, and Miss Bassett agree with her about this. Maab doesn't cry now when she comes into school, though she knows that Mrs James has kept her desk for her drawing set to one side. She also has a friend, Oona, who she loves to play with. Oona likes to do the things that Maab likes, such as make mud cakes in the playground. They have lots of fun together and really enjoy each other's company. The two girls are described as inseparable, but Mrs James and many of the other staff member don't worry about that and see it as something positive. Sometimes, Maab gets very tired at the end of the school day and likes time to herself. Mrs James is happy for her to do this since she can see that Maab is engaging in more and more learning activities during the day. She trusts that Maab knows when she wants be involved and when she needs time out and lets Maab make this decision for herself.

In thinking about Maab's experiences at school, it is possible to see that she is doing well and is able to make progress. Though some difficulties are evident, it is apparent that these are being addressed effectively. It is not simply the case, however, that a support strategy is put in place and this alone makes the difference to Maab's experience. By focusing on her relationship with her teacher, Mrs James, one can see that support for Maab exists in a number of ways. Taking the arrangement that supports Maab's transition to school in the mornings as an example, it is possible to see that other factors besides the activity of drawing are in play. Maab is fortunate enough to have a teacher who cares about her and thinks carefully about her needs, one who intuitively understands that uninterrupted time is important for her, particularly as she comes into school. Mrs James has not been put off by her initial difficulties in establishing a relationship with Maab and persists in trying to find ways of providing positive experiences of being together. Mrs James draws on different sources of knowledge, including what she has done under similar circumstances in the past as well as other people's ideas, particularly those who know Maab well. An especially important source of knowledge for Mrs James are her ongoing interactions with Maab. She tries to 'tune in' to Maab by focusing on her priorities and concerns and understanding her point of view. Mrs James finds this hard at times, but perseveres anyway. The fact that she focuses on Maab's interests and strengths is probably important. Mrs James has enough confidence in herself as a teacher to believe that she is capable of teaching Maab and can find solutions to any problems that arise.

What Mrs James believes is a critical aspect of her practice. It is apparent that she does not see Maab herself as the problem and believes that different features of the learning environment require careful consideration. Some of the actions she takes are significant, but the general ethos of her classroom and her attitude towards children are also key. She believes that children's activity in her classroom is fundamentally purposeful and in search of meaning. Finding out about how children make sense of learning situations is critically important to her role as teacher, she believes, since it allows her to know how to help them and extend their thinking. She does not see Maab as different in this respect and does not see her autism as a barrier to her learning in this way. She is supported in this, moreover, by a general culture of acceptance of difference in the school.

Though Mrs James is uncertain about how to support Maab at times, she sees this as an ordinary part of teaching and something that happens in her interactions with other children too. Learning interactions for Mrs James are about sometimes *not knowing* exactly what to say or do. Mrs James understands that interaction is an ongoing accomplishment and something she needs to pay close attention to. She continually tries to find effective ways to respond to her pupils and experiments with different ways to support them. She believes firmly in the experience of positive interactions to support children as active learners. It seems important too that Mrs James is prepared to make an adjustment for one pupil without seeing this as spoiling the experience of others. She clearly has a sense of responsibility to all the members of her class group and does not see any pupil as different in this respect.

One further feature of Maab's story we might notice is that she makes progress, but it is not possible to pinpoint precisely what brings this about. Many helpful influences and affirmative opportunities appear to be present, but few of them can be easily measured as entities that operate discretely. Rather, Maab's progress is based on an accumulation of positive experiences that are intricately linked to form a supportive learning environment. Maab benefits from a favourable interactional ecology, as Olga Solomon (2015) has described it, where she is seen as competent and where social processes are in place that allow her the opportunity to participate. Mrs James's recognition of her as a psychological agent and respect for her equal rights within communication seems crucially important in this respect. This is something that many autistic people say makes all the difference in their educational experience and what supports good outcomes. It is apparent that Maab's development reflects developments in her environment and the way in which her teacher is developing too. The growing confidence of her teacher in knowing how to support her mirrors Maab's increasing sense of safety at school and growing confidence as a learner. Maab's progress does not mean that she becomes less autistic. Rather it is the case that she is allowed to thrive in circumstances that value her as she is.

Of course, Maab's educational experience does not reflect that of many autistic pupils. It is well-documented that autistic pupils face some of the most difficult experiences in schools today. Research shows that autistic children and young people are much more likely to be excluded from school, even when compared to others with additional learning needs for whom exclusion rates are already high. Research illustrates the degree of social exclusion that exists for autistic pupils in schools and the extremely high risk of victimisation and bullying. In their systematic review of research into bullying, Neil Humphrey and Judith Hebron (2015) found that almost 90% of autistic young people in secondary schools in the UK reported being bullied at least once a week and that, in the US, 65% reported being bullied in the past year. Unsurprisingly, fewer than half of autistic pupils say they are happy in school and many say they feel they are neither understood nor adequately supported by their teachers (All Party Parliamentary Group on Autism 2017). Research finds that teachers lack confidence in their ability to support autistic pupils and experience more stress and feelings of negativity in relation to this group (Cappe et al. 2017; Roberts and Simpson 2016).

Any discussion of autism and education needs to be set against this backdrop of exclusion and unhappiness. Yet it is possible to see that the educational experience of some autistic children and young people is a good one. Though problems exist in the positivist approaches frequently used to research educational outcomes, systematic review of academic achievement suggests a high level of variability. Some children and young people are able to achieve beyond expectations, for example, and there are clear patterns of strengths in some areas (Keen et al. 2016). Similarly, achievement in a broader sense, including the attainment of qualification, employment and desired social outcomes, is found to be highly variable, with some individuals achieving good outcomes, though many falling short of this (Levy and Perry 2011). The perspectives of autistic people on their education supports this idea of variation. Many autistic writers describe positive as well as negative experiences of school, describing varied feelings about learning, teacher support, social inclusion and friendship. Very often, positive experiences of school are associated with a particularly understanding teacher who is able to establish a good relationship with the individual. William Hadcroft, in his autobiography, *The Feeling's Unmutual*, describes a mixed experience of school, with more positive experiences connected to being in the classes of teachers who he had a liking for and who in turn appreciated him as a person. He describes one such teacher, Mrs Skinner, in the following way:

> I liked her a lot too. She encouraged creativity. We all had to bring egg boxes in over a few weeks, and I marvelled as they were slowly constructed into the form of a large dragon. I thought it was amazing, and wished that I had room enough in my bedroom to make one of my own.
>
> On another occasion, she told us the story of Shadrach, Meshach and Abednego from the Bible. We were then asked to write as much of the story as we could remember. When I took my story out to Mrs Skinner, she chuckled as she read through it, impressed that I had remembered the story right down to the dialogue and had put it in.
>
> (Hadcroft 2005: 33)

In writing about autism and education, I am coming from my own perspective which is that of an academic and researcher who was once an educational practitioner. I worked for over twenty-five years in schools, sometimes teaching pupils directly, but also giving advice and support to teachers and teaching assistants. I have known many autistic pupils of all ages in different kinds of settings and I am aware that some have done well and have had good experiences of being in school. This is something that is perhaps overlooked in scholarly writings about autism and education as well as in the media, where the urgency of the difficulties some pupils face in school understandably takes precedence. But from my practical experience, I know it is possible for children and young people to make good academic progress, to feel included with their peers and be a valued member of a school community. I am saying this, not to minimise the difficulties of some pupils, but to highlight a possible way forward for all. In my research, I am concerned with empirical investigation of everyday practices that already exist to support progress for autistic pupils. In carrying out my research, I hope to achieve a better understanding of what constitutes effective pedagogy and how ordinary practitioners make sense of what they do. This book takes then a research perspective on the subject of autism and education too since I present my findings in several of the chapters as a way of illustrating what good education might look like for pupils on the spectrum.

Current debates about best practice in relation to autistic pupils tend to focus on the scaling up of specialised approaches to a more general population. The focus is one of how to transfer specialist knowledge of autism as well as knowledge about 'what works' for autistic pupils to non-specialist professional groups. General education or mainstream teachers are often described as lacking in knowledge about autism and in need of support to adopt more appropriate practices, which are mostly developed outside of general education settings. A good example of this perspective can be found in the recent recommendations of the All Party Parliamentary Group on Autism in the UK. This group endorses 'more systematic sharing of expertise between schools', which is understood as special schools 'bringing their expertise' to mainstream schools and the wider community. Recommendations include mainstream teaching assistants spending time in special school settings schools to learn about 'particular types of need' and the 'strategies to meet them' (APPGA 2017: 12). The discourse is one of transmission of knowledge about practice and the importance of specialised practices and understandings in relation to autism.

The research findings I present in this book, along with my practical experience of schools, lead me to a different conclusion however. Essentially, the arguments I set out here seek to problematise the idea that good education for autistic pupils exists in the wider dissemination of specialist knowledge and specialised practices. My research focused on young autistic pupils who are thriving within mainstream settings, that is, recognised by their teachers and parents as happy and settled in school and making good progress. The research investigated ordinary pedagogical actions taken by educational practitioners and the turn-by-turn way in which teaching and learning unfolded. Findings show that these practitioners did not see themselves as specialists in any way, but they did identify as effective educators. This identity was not associated with applying 'what works', moreover, but with a particular approach to pupil's learning. They saw virtue in trying out different pedagogical actions that were used with all pupils and in paying close attention to the ways in which a pupil responded. The role of the practitioner was described by the teachers and teaching assistants who participated in the research as one of trying to understand the ways in which a pupil was making sense within learning contexts in order to know what to offer in terms of learning support, or indeed whether support was needed. This view was framed by core beliefs about children as competent and purposeful learners who are in search of meaning. Crucially, pupils were not viewed as a set of deficits to be addressed. For some of these practitioners, aspects of autism that are typically seen as difficulties, such as communication and sociability, were seen as strengths that supported enjoyable interactions and conversations.

In carrying out the research, I realised that the educational practices I was investigating were based on a particular set of beliefs about how children learn, what good teaching involves and what development means for a human being. These beliefs in turn related to teacher identities and the broader aims of being an educational professional, as well as a particular value system in relation to the purpose of education. Decisions about what to teach and how to teach it were, I realised, always *value judgements*, that is, based on ideas about what is educationally important. The value-based nature of education is something that is seldom thought about in relation to autistic pupils, though beliefs and value systems underpin specialised practices too. Belief in education as the transmission of knowledge and skills, and the valuing of certain abilities, seen as normal and good, over other abilities, seen as problematic, pervade specialised approaches to autism. These are often presented as part of a natural order, however, with pedagogical aims and principles often not stated and rarely evaluated critically.

At this point, I want to say something briefly about the terminology I use in the book. In my arguments, I will make a clear distinction between phenomena that, in reality, probably exist in a less distinct way. The terms 'specialised' and 'specialist' and the terms 'mainstream', 'non-specialist' and 'general education' are presented as distinct phenomena, but this may not truly reflect educational realities. Some mainstream school settings host a specialist learning facility, for example, and specialist teachers go back and forth between different kinds of settings, bringing particular knowledge and specific ideas with them. In making this distinction, therefore, what I hope to draw attention to are the differences that exist between these phenomena as a set of pedagogical aims and principles, and underpinning values and beliefs. Part of my argument here concerns the fact that educators working in specialist settings and educators working in mainstream settings very often *believe they are doing different things* when they educate children and young people, including those who are autistic. They may make decisions about what actions to take based on value systems which frame different ideas about, for example, the role of the teacher, the nature of pedagogy and the purpose of education. In the chapters that follow, I will broadly contrast two value systems of relevance to a discussion of autism and education. One value system I associate with specialised practices and describe as based on a techno-rationalist model of education that constructs learners as mainly passive and pre-determined learning outcomes as possible. The other value system I examine involves beliefs about learners as active sense-makers and education as about inquiry. This could be described as a developmental model of education that many educators believe supports the most effective pedagogical practices. The idea of learning as a process is widely influential in schools today, particularly in mainstream education, and, very importantly, is seen to provide a *progressive* approach to education.

However, again it is oversimplifying the issue somewhat to make a clear distinction between sets of values and beliefs about education. It is possible, and indeed often the case, that competing values, discourses and perspectives on education exist alongside each other in a single setting. Even for one individual, conflicting ideas about practice might be drawn on at different times. By distinguishing between value systems, therefore, I am hoping to draw attention to different understandings that operate about children as learners and tensions between them. In particular, I am trying to highlight discursive practices that, on the one hand, view learning interactions as relatively unimportant and, on the other hand, as critically important and what supports the most effective educational practices. Most notably, I hope to show how some values might be seen by some educators as non-progressive, or at least, less progressive and therefore mostly irrelevant.

Two other terms I use in the book, 'educator' and 'practitioner', also require some explanation. Education is clearly broader than the idea of schooling. Education is a process of discovery that goes on outside of schools and classrooms and parents are often seen as their child's first and possibly most important educator. For the purposes of my arguments in this book, however, my use of the terms educator and educational practitioner are associated strongly with what goes on in schools. For some autistic children and young people, part of their educational experience involves intensive programmes of support that may be delivered in settings other than schools. My arguments are not focused on this form of education and type of educator or therapist, though by implication they do critique the aims, principles and underpinning value systems of some of these programmes. My arguments concern what is good education for autistic pupils *in schools*, most particularly mainstream schools, and address the question of whether schooling has anything to offer pupils on the spectrum. A central question for me is: does good education exist for autistic pupils in the same way as it does for other pupils and, if so, what does this look like.

The idea of 'good education', which is another term I use throughout the book, also needs some clarification. Gert Biesta (2010b), whose ideas centrally inform this book, points out that 'good' in relation to education is not exactly the same thing as effective. He notes that effectiveness is a technical term used to refer to the ability of processes to secure a particular outcome. He argues that it is of instrumental value, but does not describe the *ultimate value* of education. As Biesta explains, to understand the ultimate value of education we need to look beyond the immediate effectiveness of pedagogical actions and judgements and consider the moral purpose of educational practice. What is it that teachers are ultimately trying to do in respect of their pupils and what do they see as the ultimate aim of education. These are the important questions for Biesta, the answers to which determine whether education is good or not. Educational philosophy puts forward the idea that good education is ultimately concerned with providing children and young people with greater freedom. It should enable them to take full command of their abilities and to flourish in the world, but, importantly, not according to any pre-given template. Seeking to fashion young people in ways that ultimately serve the state, for example, would not constitute a good education.

In defining good education, Biesta makes the case for much greater consideration of the value-based nature of education. He sees this as a necessary antidote to the concept of evidence-based practice which, as he puts it, threatens a 'democratic deficit' within education. Evidence-based practice seeks essentially to replace teachers' professional judgement with pre-determined ideas about how to act. It tries to preempt discussions about 'the aims and ends and the conduct of education' (2010a: 492). According to Biesta, though evidence has a role to play, it should be seen as subordinate to in-depth consideration of the values that constitute good educational practices.

For Biesta and other educational philosophers there has been renewed interest in the ideas of John Dewey, who also wrote about pedagogy and the broader values of education. Dewey's liberal ideas were designed to critique education as a form of state control and focus on the way educational progress maximises individual freedoms. He took issue with a traditional view of education that prioritises the delivery of curriculum content, but also with a child-centred view of education that emphasises development as an internal process only. Dewey did not see education as concerned with unrestrained individualism, but with the interaction of the individual child and the social structures of which they are part. In his book, *Democracy and Education* (1916), and its follow up, *Experience and Education* (1938), Dewey outlined his ideas about learning as a cumulative process that emerges out of social relations within the classroom. He saw the classroom as a place where children are actively engaged with experience and in search of meaning. Children are not empty vessels waiting to be filled, according to Dewey, and what teachers know does not take precedence over what children know. Rather, good teachers engage with children on a relatively equal footing in order to be able to support a process of discovery and co-construction of knowledge. For Dewey, the personal interest of the teacher in the child and preparedness to adapt herself to what the child brings ensures a democratic order within education that ultimately supports a democratic society. What the teacher brings is a form of control, but generally a benign one that seeks to develop positive attributes in children, such as a willingness to take risks, determination to persist with a problem and a growing sense of confidence as a learner. Importantly, the teacher is viewed as developing alongside her pupils, engaged in a form of 'mutual becoming' that sees more growth in the individual pupil, but growth too in the teacher (Boyles 2018).

Dewey's ideas are seen as relevant today because they bring together important features of good education as it is presently understood. Dewey saw the curriculum as emergent out of the interactions that go on between teachers and pupils and this is especially relevant to current theorising about how children learn most effectively. In contrast to the notion of teaching as the straightforward delivery of prescribed curriculum, an emergent curriculum is much less fixed as an entity and increases the possibility of learning being meaningful and relevant. It is intimately tied up with ideas about pedagogy as the theory but also the practice of teaching. Crucially, pedagogy is defined as the use of teaching methods and translation of the curriculum in response to the ways in which pupils engage with learning. In educational theory, curriculum, pedagogy and assessment are closely interrelated since how pupils respond within learning and how teachers make assessments of this determine what is to be taught and, importantly, *how* it is taught. Teachers make momentary decisions about pupils, paying close attention to them within learning interactions. This makes the notion of complexity a critically important one for education, but also that of agency since it highlights teaching and learning as a matter of judgement and interaction.

What constitutes good education is a vital concept for a discussion of autism and education because it defines inclusive education too. Current conceptualisations of inclusive education emphasise the importance of teachers' professional judgements as they engage with individual pupils in on-going interactions in classrooms (Florian 2017). Good judgement is seen to be contingent on the teacher's core values and ability to respond equitably to the different ways in which pupils engage with learning. This has meant more focus in research on teachers' decision-making and how they enact inclusion through features of practice such as dialogue and learning relationships. Specialised practices and specialist knowledge are increasingly seen as of less importance compared to teachers' attitudes and their orientation to the different ways in which their pupils engage with learning (Black-Hawkins 2017). Inclusion as a concept for education focuses on adjustments teachers make to their own practice and understandings, more than what they do to their pupils. A change in a teacher's understanding of how a pupil is making sense, for example, is seen to lead to a profoundly altered educational experience and potentially much greater pedagogical inclusivity.

Inclusive values are strongly aligned with value-based education and ideas about children as capable learners whose search for meaning needs to be understood and engaged with by their teacher. Good education for children and young people who need extra support for their learning could thus be seen as a 'moment of relational ethics' as Dan Goodley and colleagues (2014) describe it in writing about posthuman disability studies. Inclusive education as it is currently conceived focuses on just this kind of relational space between teachers and pupils, one that is defined by individual choice-making made on a turn-by-turn basis within interactions and the understanding of the other that is accomplished in an on-going way. This is why I set out in the chapters that follow a detailed examination of what goes on between teachers and autistic pupils when they interact in classrooms. In doing this, I hope to illustrate the ways in which interaction supports the accessibility of learning for this group of pupils too. My discussion covers not only the educational experience of autistic pupils, however, but that of pupils generally as a way of exploring the question of whether good education exists in the same way for all learners.

In the next chapter I explore agency as an important concept for the emergent curriculum and for pedagogy, looking first at the agency of children. Children and young people have generally been constructed as passive learners in the literature on autism and education, but this chapter explores findings from research that demonstrate the interactional competencies of young autistic children. It is argued that such findings provide evidence of autistic children as psychological agents who make sense of the world and act according to these interpretations. This fact is then explored in relation to the concept of situated learning and the complex interplay of relational, discursive and material practices that make up an educational environment. It is argued that learning concerns increasing sophistication in the creation of meanings and connections within learning environments and relationships. An illustration of a young autistic child's experience of an educational intervention is presented finally as a way of problematising approaches to teaching and learning that overlook the inherent complexity of learning environments and the agency of children.

In Chapter 3 I turn to a discussion of the agency of teachers and explore why teachers matter in education. In this chapter, it is argued that teachers are translators of the curriculum who continually make decisions about what is to be taught in light of what their pupils know and understand. The complexity of what teachers do is described with reference to the different sources of knowledge they draw on for their practice and the ways in which they orientate themselves to their pupils and to the curriculum.

It is described how teachers try to align themselves with their pupils' states of mind and adopt different communicative approaches within pedagogy depending on what is to be taught and pupils' learning needs in relation to this. Dialogic teaching, where pupils are seen as agentive and are encouraged to question and explain, is presented as the most effective form of teaching that supports the idea of good education for many educational practitioners. In this chapter, I present findings from my research into the learning experiences of autistic pupils in mainstream schools to illustrate that such an understanding of education is relevant to this group too. Important educational experiences are described in terms of ethical practices such as the promotion of positive learner identities, and the operation of trust and respect in relationships.

Stories are used by teachers to make sense of the complexity of their practice and produce a coherent account of ideas about learning and development and the everyday realities of classrooms. Chapter 4 explores two storied versions of the curriculum that exist for autistic pupils. It is argued that one story, concerning education as essentially about recovery from autism, uses a techno-rationalist educational discourse that constructs children as passive learners. The work of Gert Biesta and other educational philosophers is drawn on to explore an alternative and more progressive vision of education that sees it as having a wider purpose, one concerned with academic learning but also personal growth and individual well-being. Two curriculum models are presented—curriculum as mastery and curriculum as process—to illustrate the ways in which progressive ideas about education are essentially incompatible with the use of specialised practices. It is argued that a focus on educational values provides an explanation of why different practices exist for autistic pupils and how mainstream practitioners think differently about their role and responsibilities in relation to this group.

In Chapter 5, I make the case for inclusive pedagogy as the approach to education that is most relevant to autistic pupils. Inclusive pedagogy assumes that all children are capable as learners and that inclusion requires change in the teacher and her beliefs, attitudes and knowledge, as well as in the context of learning. It is argued that such a view strongly aligns with the perspective of autistic people on education and their prioritisation of teacher understanding and environmental adaptation. Further critical issues for good education as it relates specifically to autistic pupils are finally outlined. These include the need for a more nuanced understanding of the role of communication within teaching and learning and proper recognition of the importance of continuous experimentation within pedagogy. Behaviour that is wrongly interpreted as non-compliant is presented as perhaps the most important issue for the education of autistic pupils, but the need for greater recognition of the professionalism of ordinary teachers and acknowledgement of existing professional standards is also raised.

In setting out my arguments for value-based education I hope to contribute to a shift away from science and towards ethics in educational policymaking for autistic pupils. This is something that Ari Ne'eman, co-founder of the Autistic Self Advocacy Network, has called for more generally. He makes the point that, though science has had an important role to play within disability policymaking, it is by focusing on values that a better vision for the future will be provided (Silberman 2012). For Ne'eman, it is in terms of ethics that the quality of services should be appraised. My arguments here seek to show how it is ethical relationships in schools that ensure quality in practice as it relates to all pupils, including those who are autistic.

References

All Party Parliamentary Group on Autism (APPGA). (2017). *Autism and education in England 2017*. London: The National Autistic Society.

Biesta, G. J. J. (2010a). Why 'what works' still won't work: From evidence-based education to value-based education. *Studies in Philosophy and Education, 29*(5), 491–503.

Biesta, G. J. J. (2010b). *Good education in an age of measurement: Ethics, politics and democracy*. London and New York: Routledge.

Black-Hawkins, K. (2017). Understanding inclusive pedagogy: Learning with and from teachers. In V. Plows & B. Whitburn (Eds.), *Inclusive education: Making sense of everyday practice* (pp. 13–30). Rotterdam: Sense Publishers.

Boyles, D. (2018). From transmission to transaction: John Dewey's imaginative vision of teaching. *Education 3-13, 46*(4), 393–401.

Cappe, E., Bolduc, M., Poirier, N., Popa-Roch, M.-A., & Boujut, E. (2017). Teaching students with autism spectrum disorder across various educational settings: The factors involved in burnout. *Teaching and Teacher Education, 67* (October), 498–508.

Dewey, J. (1916). *Democracy and education: An introduction to the philosophy of education.* New York: Macmillan.

Dewey, J. (1938). *Experience and education.* New York: Kappa Delta Pi.

Florian, L. (2017). Teacher education for the changing demographics of schooling: Inclusive education for each and every learner. In L. Florian & N. Pantić (Eds.), *Teacher education for the changing demographics of schooling: Issues for research and practice* (pp. 9–20). Dordrecht: Springer.

Goodley, D., Lawthom, R., & Runswick-Cole, K. (2014). Posthuman disability studies. *Subjectivity, 7* (4), 342–361.

Hadcroft, W. (2005). *The feeling's unmutual: Growing up with Asperger syndrome (undiagnosed).* London and Philadelphia: Jessica Kingsley Publishers.

Humphrey, N., & Hebron, J. (2015). Bullying of children and adolescents with autism spectrum conditions: A 'state of the field' review. *International Journal of Inclusive Education, 19* (8), 845–862.

Keen, D., Webster, A., & Ridley, G. (2016). How well are children with autism spectrum disorder doing academically at school? An overview of the literature. *Autism, 20* (3), 276–294.

Levy, A., & Perry, A. (2011). Outcomes in adolescents and adults with autism: A review of the literature. *Research in Autism Spectrum Disorders, 5* (4), 1271–1282.

Roberts, J., & Simpson, K. (2016). A review of research into stakeholder perspectives on inclusion of students with autism in mainstream schools. *International Journal of Inclusive Education, 20* (10), 1084–1096.

Silberman, S. (2012). Autism awareness is not enough: Here's how to change the world. In J. Bascom (Ed.), *Loud hands: Autistic people talking* (pp. 358–390). Washington, DC: The Autistic Self Advocacy Network.

Solomon, O. (2015). 'But he'll fall!': Children with autism, interspecies intersubjectivity, and the problem of 'being social'. *Culture, Medicine and Psychiatry, 39* (2), 323–344.

2

Curriculum and Pedagogy: The Child as Agent

Abstract This chapter explores agency as an important concept for teaching and learning, looking specifically at the agency of children. The chapter explores findings from research that demonstrate the interactional competencies of young autistic children and provide evidence of autistic children functioning as psychological agents. This fact is explored in relation to the concept of situated learning and the complex interplay of relational, discursive and material practices that make up a learning environment. It is argued that learning concerns increasing sophistication in the creation of meanings in relation to learning activities and pedagogical relationships. An illustration of a young autistic child's experience of an educational intervention is presented finally as a way of problematising approaches to teaching and learning that overlook the inherent complexity of learning and the agency of children.

Keywords Agency · Situated learning · Learning interactions

19

C. Conn, *Autism, Pedagogy and Education*,
https://doi.org/10.1007/978-3-030-32560-2_2

The matter of agency has become an increasingly important one in recent years as educational debates about effective pedagogy within schools have become focused on the quality of relationships and the professional judgements of teachers within learning interactions. What actions teachers take to support pupil learning and how they make decisions about this, but also the ways in which pupils make sense of and engage with learning contexts, are critical questions for any consideration of what constitutes good teaching today. This chapter and the one that follows will focus on the issue of agency, looking first at the agency of children within pedagogy. In this chapter, the notion of agency will be discussed in relation to autistic children with reference to recent research that demonstrates how children have competency as communicative agents and manage to accomplish things within social interactions. It will be illustrated how autistic children are actors who engage interactively with relational, discursive and material conditions to produce a richness of experience and social outcomes that cannot be determined beforehand. Agency will be described, not simply in terms of personal capacity and competence, but as action that arises from and is shaped by environmental conditions. It will be noted that, though this understanding of children as social actors has an important place within educational theory, it is not well understood within ideas about autism and education. By focusing on an instance of learning for a young autistic boy, I will argue that principles of practice, such as embodiment, situatedness and sense-making, are as applicable to the education of autistic pupils as they are to education more generally.

From Interaction to Enactment: Developments in Theories of Autism

It is evident that a shift has occurred at the level of policy and practice in relation to understandings about the education of autistic pupils. A narrow focus on the individual child, their biology and psychology, with change seen as needing to occur at the level of the child's behaviour, is increasingly being replaced with a wider and more encompassing view of the child in relation to their learning environment. In the UK, for example, an overview of policy and services in relation to autism emphasizes the importance of teacher training and the need for teachers to adapt their practice by developing their understanding of autism and skills in engaging pupils in learning (Parliament 2016). The shift is a profound one since viewing the child as *in relation* means always having to consider in relation *to what* and seeing that as equally of relevance in any consideration of learning and development. It means it is no longer sufficient to emphasise individual cognition since this must be viewed as part of what is being related to, with this 'what' needing to be made visible and perhaps become the focus of concern. Seeing the child as in relation opens the door to what exists around the child, such as other people and their values, understandings and expectations, how someone sees themselves in relation to different contexts and how others see them too, and the social and material environment, how it is experienced and understood.

Reasons for this shift are probably numerous. The agenda of educational inclusion is undoubtedly an important influence since it locates effective practice in the capacity of teachers to recognize and respond appropriately to the differences between learners. Inclusive education is envisaged as teachers adapting what is quite ordinary within practice by gaining a better orientation through quality assessment practices to individual pupils and what they bring to learning spaces. In addition to this educational agenda, however, the failure of psychological theories of autism to produce clarity in terms of what autism is must also be seen as contributing to a perceived need to look beyond deficit accounts of autism and a skills development approach to education. Problems with, for example, theory of mind explanations of autism arise in relation to the basic premise of modularity or separation of systems of thought (Karmiloff-Smith 2009). This computational account of the process of brain function has been replaced with more current ideas about experiential embodiment, situatedness and individual sense-making, and has prompted an interest in alternative, relational perspectives on autism (Martin and Milton 2018).

Relational perspectives on autism mark a paradigm shift by replacing the ontological view that autism is not a fixed entity that exists 'out there' with the idea that it is a social construction that gives rise to different experiences of the world. Harvey Molloy and Latika Vasil were among the first to question the pathologizing of autism by arguing that the idea of social impairment implies a 'clearly demarcated spectrum of normal social

behaviour into which all childhood behaviour confidently falls' (Molloy
and Vasil 2002: 664). They challenged whether this is really true and
put forward the idea that Asperger syndrome can never be located simply
within the individual, a fact they felt is mostly clearly demonstrated in the
high incidence of children who are seen as having a social problem only
when they first enter school. Autistic writers and activists have focused
on issues of power and personhood in relation to the social construction
of autism and questioned a dominant discourse that assumes what is 'not
autism' is part of a status quo that is unquestionably normal, natural and
good. Jim Sinclair (1993, 2013), for example, has convincingly made
the point that such a view flattens out people's personalities and unique
personal histories and reduces them to a set of inabilities to be addressed.
He has put forward the idea that such a reductionist approach does not
fully account for the formation of positive identities by autistic individuals
and the richness of people's lives. Currently, relationality as a feature of
autism is defined as the 'double empathy problem' by Damian Milton
(2012). This defines difficulty in understanding as equally experienced
by two groups of people, neurotypical and autistic, who do not share the
same outlook on the world.

In the last two decades, considerable weight to this relational view of
autism has been provided by the application in research of hitherto overlooked qualitative methodologies. These include methodologies typically
used in anthropology, interactional linguistics and sociological approaches
to interaction, perhaps most notably conversation analysis and discourse
analysis. The purpose of such research has been to discern cognitive and
interactional function (as opposed to form or 'atypical structure') of everyday communication, exploring competency in children as far as possible
rather than deficit. Barry Prizant's (1983) early work focused on echolalia
and he argued that the unusual form of children's communication, seen
as so characteristic of the condition of autism, should not give rise to the
assumption that communicative intent is necessarily absent. He thought
that the differential forms of children's communication should simply be
accepted and that investigation should focus instead on the function of
that communication within an interactional setting. Following this, studies carried out in real life situations and focusing on what is accomplished
within an interaction have found that children's neurodiverse communicative behaviour serves a range of purposes. A large number of these studies

use the method of conversation analysis since this specifically focuses on the sequence of turns between communication partners and examines what interaction manages to accomplish in terms of action. Function rather than form is key within this approach, the investigation of speaker turns used to understand how one turn follows on from another and what sense-making is taking place for individual speakers. Importantly, non-verbal communication, non-turns and delayed turns are part of the analysis and this makes the method particularly suitable for use with conversations that include autistic children and adults.

An important study by Laura Sterponi and Jennifer Shankey (2014), which extends an earlier piece of research into child-initiated reciprocal echoing behaviours in interactions between young children and their parents, analyses video recordings of real-life interactions between a five-year-old boy, Aaron, and his parents. Like other researchers using this method, Sterponi and Shankey do not isolate Aaron's echoes from the context in which they occur. Rather, they consider the placing of an echo in relation to the sequence of turns and the actions being accomplished by them. They found that Aaron used his echolalia in various ways to accomplish different things. For example, his repetition of his mother's 'one more minute' was playfully used to prolong his time in the bath and resist her command that bath-time was over. Aaron's echoes were not identical to the original utterance, however, not having the same pitch, time sequence or acoustic shape, and were used by him to manage conflict with a parent or redirect their attention away from a non-preferred action. In Extract 2.1, we see Aaron resisting his mother's insistence on a grammatically correct response by using echoes that evoke his interest in bugs and germs and make sense in the context of talk with someone who knows him well:

Extract 2.1 From Sterponi and Shankey (2014: 15)

Mom	can you make a whole sentence?
Aaron	((laughing voice)) ye:::s.
Mom	okay. let's hear it.
Aaron	((giggles)) ge:::r- ((giggling)) ge:::rms. ((croaky voice))
Mom	Roge::r is ::,
Aaron	(3.0) ger- ((laughing))
Mom	((chuckles softly))

(continued)

(continued)

Aaron	((*giggles*)) (1.0) I wanna get germs. (1.0)
Mom	you wanna get germs? okay. ((*Aaron starts walking away from the balcony and into the living room, where Mom is*))
Aaron	() wanna get ge::rms.
Mom	Aaron tell me what Roger's doing.
Aaron	no.

Extract 2.1 shows that, in using his echolalia, Aaron manages to communicate his own personal stance within a conversation and accomplish actions that are alternative to those being projected. In this way, Sterponi and Shankey conclude, Aaron demonstrates that he has agency and can act creatively according to his own priorities, ideas and interpretations. Sterponi and Shankey's study is important since it illustrates how agency exists even for a child whose communication is limited and consists partly of language that is 'borrowed' from other people. Even given these constraints, it is apparent that Aaron can *do things* with his communication, for example, he can be playful, he can tease, he can resist others and be authoritative, he can show disinterest and he can control what his parents attend to. More recent research by Terhi Korkiakangas (2018) also applies conversation analysis to interactions between an autistic child and an adult and extends this idea of the child as agent further by demonstrating how children *know* they are an agent and that their partner in communication is an agent too. In her analyses, Korkiakangas illustrates how children monitor their partner's responses to check their understanding, use gaze to prompt a response, and smiling to mark the completion of an utterance or playfully signal their intention not to respond. From the examples provided, it is possible to see within children's interactional turns that they know their partner has a different perspective on the interaction and a separate epistemic stance. Korkiakangas concludes that children's neurodiverse communication may actually be the result of preference and part of a natural communicative repertoire which 'might or might not involve gaze' (page 252), rather than the result of some kind of difficulty or indifference to social cues.

A further study of a young autistic child's interactions with his family members, this time a six-year-old boy named Barney, illustrates a further point about children's experiences of interaction. In this study, the researchers Catherine Geils and Jan Knoetze analysed video recordings of spontaneous interactions between Barney and different members of his family. They found that Barney's experience of interaction was markedly different depending on who he was interacting with and their interactional style. The researchers describe Barney's mother, for example, as having a style of interaction that is directive—what they term a 'teaching style'—whilst his father is much less directive in his communication. Compare the following two extracts. In Extract 2.2 we see Barney interacting with his mother whilst he is getting dressed and in Extract 2.3 he is pond dipping with his father:

Extract 2.2 From Geils and Knoetze (2008: 207)

Mom:	Yes some underpants good what colour underpants are you wearing today? (3.17) what colour underpants you wearing today (2.99) tell me what colour underpants
Barney:	((B putting on underpants)) ((Turns back towards cupboard - grunts))
Mom:	I'm a:sking you a question
Barney:	(1.62) pants
Mom:	what colour underpants are you wearing (2.69) mm
Barney:	((Grunts)) ((Lying back on bed))
Mom:	what colour underpants are you wearing (1.09)
Barney:	((half turns towards M)) ↑blue↑

Extract 2.3 From Geils and Knoetze (2008: 208–209)

Dad:	come go get that net and we'll stick it in
Barney:	((turns around and looks in direction of net, then runs to fetch net)) I oh et the net (.) I odit I odit I odit I odit (.) ow ((as he lays the net on the ground))
Dad:	ow

(continued)

(continued)

Barney:	I ((picks up tube)) odit I odit ((holds the tube over the water)) (2)
Dad:	throw it
Barney:	((drops it in the water)) and is ↑in↑ the tower
Dad:	get the net
Barney:	shoo::ee ((fetches net and dips it in the pool)) ((singing)) ((scoops out the tube, puts net down on the grass))
Dad:	come pick it up (2.32) Barney come pick it up (2.19) ((D and B hold the pole of the net together, D standing behind B))
Dad:	let's catch the bugs (.) catch a bugs (4) come catch a bugs (9) >here y'are ((hands B the tube)) >throw it in again<
Barney:	((takes the tube and throws it in the water))

The different interaction styles of Barney's mother and father are clearly evident with his mother taking an authoritative stance and repeating her question in an insistent way. Barney's father, by contrast, uses a less authoritative and softer manner—what Geils and Knoetze describe as a nurturing style—that appears to be more effective as a form of communication. Barney's father issues instructions but in a way that accepts the form that Barney's communication takes, even mimicking it at times. It is apparent that the experience of interaction is very different in the two extracts, with differing levels of participation evident, including differences in attentiveness, motivation and energy, as well as levels of enjoyment and the existence of different identities, roles and relationships (for his dad, Barney is a helper). However, as Geils and Knoetze point out, it is not simply the case that Barney's father demonstrates more effective communicative behaviour than his mother. This is too simplistic an analysis and overlooks the way in which each interaction is configured in terms of its salient features. In Extract 2.3, it is apparent that it is the configuration of activity, purpose, object of interest (bugs), pond, net, child-adult relationship, identity *and* the way in which language is used that together produce an enjoyable experience of interaction. It is this configuration in its entirety that shapes how Barney thinks, acts and responds. Equally, in Extract 2.2, the differential style of Barney's mother and different experience of interaction might be explained by the configuration of features that are active in this situation. These include the reason for getting dressed, the mother's confidence in the effectiveness of her communication, Barney's possibly resistant stance, his mother's cumulative experience of interaction with Barney over time, her ideas about parenting and her ideas about autism.

Consideration of Barney's experience allows us to see that the organizing principle within social interaction is not the inner cognitive processes of each individual in an event, but rather *the interaction itself,* how it is configured, presents itself to the people involved and unfolds. Barney and his father do not simply act upon their environment since their environment clearly asserts an influence over them too. In Extract 2.3, the material features of pond, net and bugs suggest actions to be carried out, but also have an energy of their own that adds dynamism to the interaction and helps to invest it with its quality of nurturing. This extract serves to remind us that social interaction is an open-ended system that is, importantly, not a pre-given fact. People are social actors who perceive affordances within their environment, make personal sense of these and act according to their interpretations, but *things* also suggest possible actions to people and draw them in. Patterns of behaviour are discernible in events that are similar in nature, but these are not prescribed and do not dictate necessarily what people do, how they feel and what they know.

Unsurprisingly, findings such as these have led some to argue that an enactive approach to cognition is as relevant for describing the engagement of autistic people as it is for all people. An enactive approach views cognition not as a fixed and representational state of mind, but as an externally directed process—an enactment—that is related to how environments are configured, made sense of and temporally evolve. The idea of enactment is seen as best suited to describing the highly interrelated and mutually constituting nature of personal experience, embodiment, sense-making, the affordances and constraints that are actively present for the individual in a given situation, and the emergence of action and consequence as a coherent part of this. In critiquing psychological theories of autism and making the case for an enactive approach to cognition, Hanne De Jaegher (2013) argues that how the individual connects with their lifeworld and 'casts a web of significance' must be seen as of consequence, but also how actions take on a life of their own and in part create the intentions of those engaged. Consideration of enactment as a basis of cognition has supported alternative explanations of autism developed by people who are themselves autistic. Dinah Murray et al. (2005) have developed the concept of monotropism to describe the way in which attention and personal interest connect with a single sense dominated system to produce a particular mode of interaction with the environment. In her book, *The Passionate Mind*, Lawson makes the case for an innovative theory of autistic cognition, Single Attention and Associated Cognition in Autism, based on the concept of monotropism. This seeks to account for common patterns of behaviour, cognition and emotion in terms of neurodiverse brain configuration and the single channeling of information. Associated concepts focused on experiences of constraint in terms of motor control, such as sensory overload and autistic inertia, are similarly used to describe the disconnect that often exists between intention and the non-emergence of action that operates for some people (Unstrange Mind 2016). More will be said below about people as actors and enactment as a way of thinking about what happens when autistic children participate in learning situations, but first I will turn to developments within the field of education and how there is increasing interest here too in children's engagement with the material world.

Socio-Materiality and Learning: Developments in the Field of Education

Within the field of education, the idea that children have agency and make sense of and actively engage with their worlds is deeply embedded within ideas about learning and educational practice. Different approaches to learning exist, but a social constructivist view of learning has been profoundly influential on the development of educational policy and practice in the last three decades, particularly within Western societies. A social constructivist approach to learning emphasizes the cultural resources that are available within specific contexts and how these are made sense of and used by children as learners. Importantly, these resources include the teacher who is seen as having a critical role to play in terms of extending learning and taking children beyond what they already know and can do. As James Gee (2008) and others have argued, situated learning is not concerned with mental representations in the heads of individual children, but rather focuses on the relationship between the embodied learner, their environment and the distributed knowledge that exists across individuals, tools, texts and technologies. There is emerging consensus that effective forms of educational support for the development of cognition involve engagement in 'social modes of thinking' (Mercer 2000) which prioritise pupil participation and promote pupil enquiry. In such learning spaces, new ideas are embraced, difference is respected and seen as of value, and pupils' subjectivities are open to negotiation. Children as learners are understood to have a present state of understanding which can be developed through relationships and dialogue with their teachers and actions performed in a range of learning environments. In the UK, the largest initiative in educational research in recent years, the Teaching and Learning Research Programme (TLRP), coordinated 70 research projects covering all aspects of education from early years to higher education and workplace learning, and developed ten general principles for effective teaching and learning from its findings. These principles are overwhelmingly social constructivist in nature with eight out of ten directly addressing social processes, active engagement and the importance of personal ways of knowing (James and Pollard 2011).

In the last decade, theorising about situated learning has sought to probe beyond what is available through language and human relationships and conceptualise more fully the bodily experience of learning experiences for children. Interest has become focused on the importance of *things* in thinking about the social within situated learning. An approach to education which has been variously described as socio-materiality or 'the new materialism' has introduced ideas about the 'vitality of matter' in children's learning experiences and the materiality of embodied participation in educational contexts (Edwards and Fenwick 2015). Learning spaces are described as existing as networks of associations where the human and nonhuman come together in moments of significance for children, teachers and others. Theorists of early childhood education, for example, take a keen interest in embodied learning, the many ways young children engage with learning spaces, and the array of material artefacts and other matter available to them. In making the case for an approach to education that seeks to engage more readily with the complexity, diversity and non-reducible nature of learning spaces—what she terms as 'relational materialism'—Hellevi Lenz Taguchi (2011) describes a moment of engagement for a young girl as she plays with sand in a sandbox. In the photograph that is provided we see the little girl playing with great concentration, but Lenz Taguchi asks a question about what we *do not see*. The girls pours sand in a stream from her fist, but as Lenz Taguchi points out, we do not and cannot see the soft, grainy sand evoking in the child a desire to slowly let it run out of her grasp with increasing speed and fall into the red bucket below. Lenz Taguchi writes:

> In this way it would be relevant to ask: Is the girl playing with the sand or is the sand playing with the girl?…We think that the playing is taking place *in-between* [emphasis in original] the girl and the sand. We contend that there is no clear border between them in this event. The force of the girl's body and the force of the sand overlap and extend onto and into each other. Each change in either of them will resonate in the other. Agency and intentionality are thus considered to be distributed among several performative agents…The differences between the sand and the girl are thus not fixed, absolute or inherent.
>
> (Lenz Taguchi 2011: 37–38)

As Lenz Taguchi points out, it is clear from the photograph that girl and sand are actively doing something together, but what is much less clear is the way in which the sand—through the exertion of its force on the hand of the girl and into the sandbox—asks questions of the girl. Questions might include the following: how must the girl balance in order to carry out the action, what is the correct height of her hand to achieve a satisfying stream of sand, how much does she need to open her fist in order to release the sand at the right speed. Lenz Taguchi notes that the girl:

> directs her whole body around the sand and what the sand forces her to do in relation to the uneven foundation in the sandbox and the quality of the grains of sand. These are all active forces that interact with her body and mind and that she has to work with and against. The girl as a learning subject emerges and becomes-with the sand in the sandbox, and the sand becomes-with the girl.
>
> (Lenz Taguchi 2011: 38)

Lenz Taguchi draws the conclusion that girl, sand and bucket are each a performative agent and form an 'assemblage of forces and flows' that produce a valuable learning interaction. She and others note, however, that the inability to perceive the material aspects and productions of this coming together has led to the dominance of an anthropocentric view of learning and cognition, one that sees human intention, motivation, disposition and understanding as always the prime or sole mover in events. By contrast, Lenz Taguchi presents a non-hierarchical view of interaction, one that sees mind, body, relationship *and* material conditions as equally having the potential to exert force, to dominate at any point and determine how interactions unfold.

A socio-material approach to education draws on the work of posthumanists such as Gilles Deleuze, Félix Guattari and Donna Haraway, but it is perhaps the writings of Karen Barad that are most influential within education currently. Her book, *Meeting the Universe Halfway: Quantum Physics and the Entanglement of Matter and Meaning*, which explores quantum physics and the nature of matter and meaning, critiques a view of the world that presents it as a series of binary opposites, for example, human-nonhuman, cultural-natural, objective-subjective, scientific-everyday, representational-material. Barad makes a case against the idea of the separatedness of human beings from things 'out there', that is, against the Cartesian idea of a knowing subject that exists separately from external objects. Barad puts forward a non-hierarchical view of the human and the nonhuman that does not view one as more superior, active or intentional than the other, but posits difference as inherent in the comparative visibility of each and ability to articulate experience. For Barad, the concept of representationalism, that is so central to the humanist thinking she critiques, is problematic since it 'brackets out' the material aspects of practices that produce what is being represented. In order to create boundaries around things and identify discrete entities, notions of 'girl' 'mind' and 'sand'—to use the example provided above—are developed in order to allow us to see and describe these things, but not the *doings* that are going on between them and what is produced. Barad argues that representationalism creates the (false) impression that something is a thing in itself, that is, separate from everything else. According to Barad, representation essentially makes a 'cut' which includes some aspects of phenomena whilst excluding others, but this glosses over the deeply connected, inter-dependent entanglement of human and nonhuman matter and meaning. Barad maintains that notions of being, identity, matter, causality, agency, dynamics and discourse need to be radically re-thought and coins the word *intra*-action to describe the inseparability of agents and the fact that 'we make knowledge not from the outside but as part of the world' (Barad 2007: 91). For Barad, it is attention to the fine details of experiences that is crucial since this allows the iterative production of reality through intra-action to be seen, including the ways in which people know and understand the world.

Socio-materiality puts forward the idea that embodiment, action and experience cannot be separated out from one another and together support cognition and learning. Lenz Taguchi points out too that it is impossible to separate knowing from being in children's learning and that thinking and talking should not be seen as different or more desirable to embodied doing. Children's continual intra-actions support ongoing learning in different contexts. They are performative agents who encounter other performative agents, of both the human and nonhuman kind, and come together with these to 'enact matter within practices of knowing' (Barad 2007: 91). Development in children should not be seen as a matter of increasing independence of mind, but rather the growing ability to make connections between things and create meanings in relation to these. Importantly, as children engage in different assemblages of the human and nonhuman within learning environments, they develop and extend their identities as learners as they do so, for example, competency in relation to numbers visually organized and patterned, or enjoyment and excitement in relation to swings, slides and roundabouts in the playground. Such experiences circumscribe future states of being, prompt performative actions and support further knowing or learning.

Though the focus of this discussion thus far has been on young children and situated learning within early childhood education, socio-materiality should not be seen as any less descriptive of learning within the later years. In fact, prominent educational theorists who have proposed socio-materiality as an approach to thinking about teaching and learning, such as Tara Fenwick and Richard Edwards, have developed their ideas in relation to adult education (see, for example, Fenwick et al. 2011). The material opportunities and constraints of all learning environments are seen as constitutive of educational experience and the development of learning identities. For students studying a hospitality college course within upper secondary and further education settings, Edwards (2012) shows how the same unit descriptors in relation to the prescribed curriculum are enacted by two lecturers in different ways. One uses the material circumstances of a professional-type kitchen classroom environment and work-wear as well as groupings, technologies and texts to enact teaching learners who are valued, responsible and able to achieve professionally, whilst the other enacts teaching as a matter of control and behaviour management. For Edwards and other academics interested in socio-material theories, the discursive practices of teachers are not seen as independent of material circumstances. Rather there is an intimate relation between what is said to count and have meaning, and by implication, what does not count and is excluded. Discursive practices produce rather than merely describe the world so that matter and meaning, concepts and materiality are tightly bound up together (Barad 2007: 147).

Socio-materiality as an approach to education is not without its critics with problems seen to arise in relation, not only to the complexity of related theories, but to an inherent apoliticism. Callum McGregor (2014) has argued that the 'new materialism' does not appear to be different in any way from other materialisms, such as Marxian historical materialism, which also theorises material reality, its dynamics and how power is enacted through spatial-material arrangements. McGregor argues that the strong focus on nonhuman agency and intentionality in the new materialism is its only distinguishing feature, but sees this as creating a multiplicity of connections and assemblages that mean 'we never leave the local level' and are less likely to take political action. For those of us working in the area of autism and education, however, it will be apparent that an approach to learning which seeks to conceptualise engagement with matter and the material in an equal way to language and human relationships holds an appeal. This is not to say that language and human relationships are not important features of education for autistic learners, but the 'liveliness of objects' is something that many autistic writers emphasise. Many writers describe their relationship with objects as being one that is associated with feelings of connectedness, well-being and sense-making, the objects themselves presented as holding more power and meaning for some individuals than relationships with human beings (Higashida 2013; Mukhopadhyay 2008). Embodiment is increasingly seen as a way of thinking about autism as a condition, with neurodiverse experiences of embodiment—that are more sensorily and perceptually based—underpinning the different ways in which autistic people engage, learn and develop. With this in mind, I will turn finally to a consideration of curriculum and pedagogy as it is envisaged for autistic pupils, exploring once again issues of agency and socio-materiality, this time in relation to a prominent feature of the discourse of autism and education: the concept of intervention.

Children's Agency and the Concept of Educational Intervention

The use of interventions with autistic adults and children has become somewhat of a mantra within policy documents and curriculum guidance, though Damian Milton (2014) has questioned the underlying purpose of these and whether the aim to change people's nature and methods used to do this raise significant ethical issues. The idea of using interventions is aligned with the agenda of evidence-based practice which continues to exert a strong influence over the area of autism and education, but also inclusive education and education more generally. Evidence-based practice refers to the idea that professionals working in education and other services should base their practice on the best available evidence about what is effective for the particular group with whom they are working. Evidence is most often conceptualized as knowledge that has been gained in specific ways, usually through transparent research designs that are based on scientific methods, such as randomized control trials. The idea is that knowledge about 'what works' can be determined in a rigorous and robust way and then transferred to similar populations. Such a notion of practice continues to influence thinking about autism and education profoundly. The clarity of this kind of techno-rationalist model of education—to find out what works and apply that—holds a natural appeal. Researchers seek to establish the effective components of an intervention which is then envisaged as being delivered by teachers who faithfully follow a set of precise instructions. This kind of discourse borrows from a medicalised view of learning that reduces the child, the teacher and pedagogical practice to a set of modular components that can be individually controlled, enhanced or eliminated, much like the treat-and-trial methods of Western medicine. Many approaches to autism and learning continue to use a discourse of locating a problem, such as a skill or knowledge 'gap', and then delivering a programme, treatment or intervention to address only this.

Problems with this account were set out in Martyn Hammersley's (2005) seminal critique of evidence-based practice as a model for education. This makes the point that pedagogical practice, and professional practice more generally within public services, must be seen as a matter of judgement rather than the straightforward application of knowledge. Within education, teachers draw on different sources of ideas, information and priorities in making context-sensitive, moment-to-moment decisions about their pupils and what they bring to pedagogical spaces. Hammersley argues that evidence-based practice presents too simplistic an idea of causality in education—that 'treatment' of children can result in a pre-determined outcome—and shows misunderstanding of what learning actually is. In order to make the idea of evidence-based practice workable, a very significant 'cut', to use Barad's term, has to be made in terms of what teaching and learning is understood to be, and what must be bracketed as outside of this. For an intervention to exist as a thing in itself, that is, as something that simply needs to be administered with precision, what is outside of teaching and learning includes a breathtakingly large number of factors. These include, not only judgement and sense-making, but also relationship, discourse, identity, embodiment and materiality for teachers and pupils, and in addition for teachers, professional development and accountability. Pedagogy takes place in the space between teachers and pupils and is contingent on principles of practice, educational values and ideas about what is to be learned. It is also dependent on immediate features within learning environments, such as the quality of relationships and the way in which learning interactions unfold. The outcomes of pedagogical actions and interactions are not pre-given and learning can never be delivered exactly as planned. As Gert Biesta (2013) has so forcefully argued, education is a weak endeavor, teachers presenting ideas and issues with the knowledge that they cannot fully control the impact of these on their pupils. As Biesta describes it, education is a 'beautiful risk' and teachers go about their work with close attention to their relationships with their pupils and the ways in which what they have to offer is received. This is something that teachers understand from their daily interactions with pupils, but not necessarily what researchers understand who operate outside of school settings. These ideas are so central to my arguments in this book that I will return to them again in Chapter 4.

To demonstrate this point about education in relation to autistic pupils, an exercise I often do with the Masters students I teach is to watch online videoclips that demonstrate 'excellence in educational practice' for autistic children. The idea is to encourage students to think about the underlying principles of individual approaches, but also to consider whether an approach in practice really is what it says it is. As a way of gaining different perspectives on learning, I ask students to consider the experience of pedagogy from the point of the view of the teacher—or therapist in some instances—and then again from the point of view of the child. I particularly like to use an online clip that shows the enthusiastic engagement of a young autistic boy in an applied behaviour analysis (ABA) treatment session, an approach to autism that aims to produce an observable change in social and communicative behaviour through a system of reinforcements. The clip is especially good at demonstrating how social and material features of learning environments organize children's experiences temporally and emotionally and an extended description of the three and half minute clip is set out below:

A five-year-old boy and his male therapist sit on low chairs facing one another in a treatment room, with small play objects set out on a table beside them. In the written information that accompanies the clip, it is explained that the boy is engaged in learning a new skill in pretend play, that is, to respond appropriately to requests to make toy animals perform actions within a pretend play scene. At the beginning of the clip, the therapist first establishes what kind of motivating reward the boy wants for that session. He gives him the option of walking, jumping or running, using his hands on the boy's legs to carry out each of these actions, accompanied by appropriate vocalisations (e.g. 'walk – walk – walk' said slowly, and 'run-run-run' said very fast). The boy quickly says, "Run!", and the therapist does this action on the boy's legs, moving them very fast. The therapist is a large and strong man and he performs the actions vigorously, making the boy laugh out loud. They spend a few moments doing this – running vigorously (the therapist doing this to the boy's legs) and then stopping and the therapist saying "We get so tired!", and then getting ready to run again. The boy orientates himself to the therapist throughout, anticipating what he is about to do and repeating back some of his words with a smile. The boy then asks for a balloon pump by holding out the sleeve of his jumper. The therapist replies, "Yeah, I've got it", showing him the pump, but first asks him to do something else. He says, "First, you've got to do this okay. Make the cat run", holding up one of the small toy animals on the table. The boy looks at the therapist as he runs the cat toy along the side of the table, and then takes the toy and repeats the action himself, doing this more as a tapping of the toy on one spot on the table. As the boy does this, the therapist quickly gets the balloon pump ready and then puts it up the boy's sleeve, the boy holding out his sleeve when he has finished with the cat toy. The therapist pumps air up the boy's sleeve, quietly at first as the boy giggles. Then he takes hold of the boy and lifts him into the air as if he is a balloon rising up, his voice getting louder all the time. The therapist is tall and the boy goes high into the air, giggling all the time. The therapist then says, "Oh the balloon's going to pop!" and then wiggles the boy's body as he brings him back down to his chair, the boy giving a satisfied chuckle as he lands back on it. The therapist asks the boy again to make the cat run, going back to the toys on the table, and the boy again quickly taps the toy on the table. The therapist then shakes the boy's hand in a comical way, making his arm wobble forcefully as he repeats, "Thank you very much. Thank you very much". The boy laughs and immediately holds out his sleeve for the balloon pump, but the therapist instructs him first to perform two actions saying, "Make the cat run", and then, "Make the cow run". The boy does this very quickly and then says clearly, "I want to play the balloon". The therapist gives the boy a few more instructions and then picks up the balloon pump. This time he starts off slowly, pumping air up the boy's sleeve whilst making 'sshh-sshh-sshh' pumping sounds, the boy giggling delightedly in anticipation. Then he lifts the boy up very high, holding him for a brief while as they smile at each other before bringing him down, the boy laughing loudly now and slapping his thighs with pleasure as he sits back down.

This session could clearly be described as successful in terms of the boy's attention to what is going on and in his interactions with the therapist. The boy is orientated towards the therapist throughout, anticipates what is going to happen and is fully engaged. He responds correctly to almost all the therapist's instructions, the therapist showing his appreciation of this by blowing up the sleeve of the boy's jumper towards the end while the boy laughs and wriggles away. It is a hugely enjoyable clip to watch and when it is finished I ask my students what the child has learned, taking the point of view of the therapist. Invariably, they point out that the boy is very engaged in the session, but are usually unsure whether it is possible to conclude that he has learned to carry out pretend play, or indeed if his actions with the toys have any meaning for him at all. I ask them then to consider the session again, but this time from the child's point of view and describe what he has learned. This shifts the focus onto the reward part of the session and the boy's delight in the sensory and physical actions of the therapist. Students may mention the fact that the boy has had an experience of playful interaction with another person, of being lifted very high in the air and of repeating requests for more of same. The discussion usually comes round to the fact that the focus of learning for the child—and indeed for the therapist who puts much more effort into the reward actions—is not behaviour relating to pretend play or verbal instruction, but engagement within physically playful interaction and all that this involves. I point out that by focusing on the reward actions, which make up the bulk of the clip, this session would in fact qualify to be some other form of intervention used with autistic children. Sometimes I show students a specific Youtube clip of an Intensive Interaction session, an approach to autism that shares none of the educational principles of ABA. Intensive Interaction focuses on the 'fundamentals of communication' by finding positive and meaningful child-centred ways of relating, but in this Intensive Interaction clip the same configuration of important features operate as in the ABA clip, that is, two people, air, blowing and joyful interaction. From the point of view of the autistic learner in each instance, it could easily be the case that little or no difference exists in their learning experience.

   The point I am trying to make here is that a teacher, therapist, researcher or institution might declare that an intervention is something, but whether this really is the case depends on the way in which interactions are configured in a particular time and place. Principles of practice and beliefs about what is to be learned will make up only part of this configuration, with relationships, activity, material realities, motivations and expectations probably also playing an important role. What I am talking about here is not simply 'therapist drift' as defined by Rita Jordan and Stuart Powell (1996) in relation to therapeutic interventions used with autistic children. Instead, I am making the case for consideration of children's sense-making and agency to any context of learning. The boy in the ABA clip knows nothing of behaviourism, pivotal response and mass trials. These are not things in his head as he engages so intently with his therapist. The energy and enthusiasm with which the therapist carries out the reward actions would suggest that they are not prominent considerations for him either within the session. The responses of the little boy are crucially important since his agency and joyous engagement with the salient features of the scene—balloon pump, air, an exciting play partner who can lift him high up in the air—exert huge energy within the interaction. The fact that the material features of this learning context support the kind of sensory and physical playfulness that is so appealing to many autistic children is a further important point of course. In the clip, the boy is determining as much as his therapist how his learning temporally unfolds. Students coming from an educational background, particularly a mainstream education background, tend to understand this point well. Their training, practice and continuing professional development encourages the stance that children have agency as learners and that valuable learning comes out of embodied experiences of the environment, material things and interactions with other people, particularly when the child is emotionally engaged. Educational professionals working in schools tend to understand that teaching practice centrally involves sensitive engagement with children's subjectivities as actors within learning contexts. Recommendations about practice that are regularly made within the academic literature on autism seem mostly unable, however, to grasp this fact. The discourse is relentlessly one of pedagogy as a means-ends approach: do x intervention and y will happen, do p and q will be learned. The discourse of autism and education does not allow for any pause to consider whether x is actually x

as taught in this setting or whether something other than q has been unexpectedly learned. There has been little consideration too whether the idea of intervention as it is often conceived in specialist discourses of autism reflects anything that operates in actual classrooms.

It is evident, in fact, that researchers and educators—perhaps especially those working in non-specialist settings—hold different and probably irreconcilable ideas about fundamental educational issues. Their perspectives on what is a child, what is a teacher and what is learning often seem highly opposed. Different ideas about pedagogy and the curriculum often exist for these two groups, with educational practitioners taking a broader, more process-driven view of what is to be learned. They see this as part of the whole school experience, inside and outside of the classroom, through the delivery of lesson content, but also through positive relationships, in the ethos and culture of the school, and in the way in which the school engages with families and the local community. More will be said about the divergence that exists in competing discourses of autism and education in Chapter 4. Before this, I will explore the issue of agency within education further, but this time focusing on the actions of teachers.

References

Barad, K. (2007). *Meeting the universe halfway: Quantum physics and the entanglement of matter and meaning.* Durham and London: Duke University Press.

Biesta, G. J. J. (2013). *The beautiful risk of education.* Abingdon, Oxon and New York: Routledge.

De Jaegher, H. (2013). Embodiment and sense-making in autism. *Frontiers in Integrative Neuroscience, 7*(15), 1–14.

Edwards, R. (2012). Translating the prescribed into the enacted curriculum in college and school. In T. Fenwick & R. Edwards (Eds.), *Researching education through actor-network theory* (pp. 23–39). Chichester, West Sussex: Wiley-Blackwell.

Edwards, R., & Fenwick, T. (2015). Critique and politics: A sociomaterialist intervention. *Educational Philosophy and Theory, 47*(13–14), 1385–1404.

Fenwick, T., Edwards, R., & Sawchuk, P. (2011). *Emerging approaches to educational research: Tracing the socio-material*. Abingdon, Oxon and New York: Routledge.

Gee, J. (2008). A sociocultural perspective on opportunity to learn. In P. A. Moss, D. C. Pullin, J. P. Gee, E. H. Haertel, & L. J. Young (Eds.), *Assessment, equity, and opportunity to learn* (pp. 76–108). Cambridge, New York, Melbourne, Madrid, Cape Town, Singapore, São Paulo, and New Delhi: Cambridge University Press.

Geils, C., & Knoetze, J. (2008). Conversations with Barney: A conversation analysis of interactions with a child with autism. *South African Journal of Psychology, 38*(1), 200–224.

Hammersley, M. (2005). Is the evidence-based practice movement doing more good than harm? Reflections on Iain Chalmers' case for research-based policy making and practice. *Evidence and Policy: A Journal of Research, Debate and Practice, 1*(1), 85–100.

Higashida, N. (2013). *The reason I jump: One boy's voice from the silence of autism* (K. A. Yoshida & D. Mitchell, Trans.). London: Sceptre.

James, M., & Pollard, A. (2011). TLRP's ten principles for effective pedagogy: Rationale, development, evidence, argument and impact. *Research Papers in Education, 26*(3), 275–328.

Jordan, R., & Powell, S. (1996). Therapist drift: Identifying a new phenomenon in evaluating therapeutic approaches. In G. Linfoot & P. Shattock (Eds.), *Therapeutic intervention in autism* (pp. 21–30). Sunderland: Autism Research Centre, University of Sutherland.

Karmiloff-Smith, A. (2009). Nativism versus neuroconstructivism: Rethinking the study of developmental disorders. *Developmental Psychology, 45*(1), 56–63.

Korkiakangas, T. K. (2018). *Communication, gaze and autism: A multimodal interaction perspective*. London and New York: Routledge.

Lenz Taguchi, H. (2011). Investigating learning, participation and becoming in early childhood practices with a relational materialist approach. *Global Studies of Childhood, 1*(1), 36–50.

Martin, N., & Milton, D. (2018). Supporting the inclusion of autistic children. In G. Knowles (Ed.), *Supporting inclusive practice and ensuring opportunity is equal for all* (pp. 111–124). Abingdon, Oxon: Routledge.

McGregor, C. (2014). From social movement learning to sociomaterial movement learning? Addressing the possibilities and limits of new materialism. *Studies in the Education of Adults, 48*(2), 211–227.

Mercer, N. (2000). *Words and minds: How we use language to think together*. London: Routledge.

Milton, D. E. M. (2012). On the ontological status of autism: The 'double empathy problem'. *Disability and Society, 27*(6), 883–887.

Milton, D. E. M. (2014). So what exactly are autism interventions intervening with? *Good Autism Practice, 15*(2), 6–14.

Molloy, H., & Vasil, L. (2002). The social construction of Asperger syndrome: The pathologising of difference? *Disability and Society, 17*(6), 659–669.

Mukhopadhyay, T. R. (2008). *How can I talk if my lips don't move?* New York: Arcade Publishing.

Murray, D., Lesser, M., & Lawson, W. (2005). Attention, monotropism and the diagnostic criteria for autism. *Autism, 9*(2), 139–156.

Parliament. House of Commons. (2016, April 21). *Autism—Overview of UK policy and services* (Briefing Paper CBP 07172). London: House of Commons Library. Available at: https://researchbriefings.parliament.uk/ResearchBriefing/Summary/CBP-7172. Accessed 2 November 2018.

Prizant, B. (1983). Language acquisition and communicative behavior in autism: Toward an understanding of the 'whole' of it. *Journal of Speech and Hearing Disorders, 48*(3), 296–307.

Sinclair, J. (1993). Don't mourn for us. *Our Voice*, Autism Network International Newsletter, 1(3). Available at: https://www.autreat.com/dont_mourn.html. Accessed 1 November 2018.

Sinclair, J. (2013). Why I dislike 'person first' language. *Autonomy, the Critical Journal of Interdisciplinary Autism Studies, 1*(2). Available at: http://www.larry-arnold.net/Autonomy/index.php/autonomy/article/view/OP1/pdf. Accessed 1 November 2018.

Sterponi, L., & Shankey, J. (2014). Rethinking echolalia: Repetition as interactional resource in the communication of a child with autism. *Journal of Child Language, 41*(2), 275–304.

Unstrange Mind. (2016, October 7). *Autistic inertia: An overview.* Available at: http://unstrangemind.com/autistic-inertia-an-overview/. Accessed 24 April 2019.

3

Curriculum and Pedagogy: The Teacher as Agent

Abstract This chapter focuses on the agency of teachers and explores the ways in which teachers make decisions about what to teach in light of how their pupils respond. The complexity of what teachers do is described with reference to different sources of knowledge they draw on for their practice and the ways in which they orientate themselves to their pupils and to the curriculum. How teachers adopt different communicative approaches within pedagogy is described with reference to the concept of dialogic teaching. This is presented as the most effective approach to pedagogy, one that sees pupils as agentive and supports the idea of a good education. Case study examples of the learning experiences of autistic pupils in mainstream schools are used to illustrate the relevance of this approach to this group.

Keywords Teacher agency · Pedagogy · Knowledge sources

The agenda of inclusion is now two decades old, but it nevertheless continues to fuel debates about appropriate forms of education and support for children and young people who experience difficulty with learning. Rather than a straightforward matter of mainstreaming pupils, inclusion is viewed increasingly in terms of dimensionality, that is, the ways in which children and young people feel themselves to be included and able to participate in learning activities, roles and relationships in schools (Qvortrup and Qvortrup 2018). From the perspective of teachers, the understanding that teaching for some pupils is a matter of delivering individualized instruction focused on the remediation of skills has shifted in favour of a more equitable approach. Inclusive education is seen much more as requiring a particular mind-set by teachers, and indeed peers and the whole school community, as opposed to a set of pedagogical practices that are specialised or different in some way (Florian 2017). In current conceptualisations of inclusive pedagogy, all pupils are seen as having agency as learners and as active in the construction of personal knowledge. All are seen as capable of learning, but an important condition in this are positive experiences of participation for the pupil and the development of a sense of belonging (Hart and Drummond 2013). Academic learning and the experience of personal relationships are highly inter-related in this respect, with both viewed as foundational for good educational outcomes (Biesta 2009). This makes the cooperative actions of peers an important issue, but also the actions of teachers and the relational space in which teachers and pupils exist. Inclusive practice resides in the momentary judgements of teachers as they engage with individual pupils in on-going interactions in classrooms and other learning spaces, with good judgement contingent upon the teacher's ability to recognize and respond appropriately to the different ways in which pupils engage with learning (Florian and Graham 2014).

That teachers matter for inclusion reflects the wider recognition that teachers matter generally within education. In the editorial to a special issue of the *Journal of Curriculum Studies* focused on the work of teachers, Daniel Alvunger and colleagues (2017) note that current educational policy clearly recognizes teachers as the most important resource for school improvement and ensure equity of access to the curriculum for all pupils. Their depiction of teachers as the link between educational policy and the everyday context of the classroom is an important one since it emphasizes the balancing act teachers must engage in to manage competing interests and concerns. Teachers are neither programmable devices to deliver prescribed curriculum nor do they see themselves as fully autonomous and free to make unilateral decisions about children's learning. Instead, they are authors of the curriculum—curriculum-makers as David Lambert and Mary Biddulph (2015) have put it in writing about the progressive curriculum—who enact pedagogy and transform specified aspects of the curriculum, but always in consideration of the agency of their pupils and the educational priorities of their settings. Teaching could be characterised as the continual making of judgements about what is to be taught (curriculum goals) in the light of what pupils already understand and how they engage. Within the triumvirate of teacher, pupil and the curriculum, an over- or under-emphasis on one aspect will lead to a breakdown of pedagogical practice. An over-emphasis on what is to be learned, for example, without consideration of the interests and experiences of pupils, may lead to apathy or resistance on the part of the pupil. Conversely, an over-emphasis on what the pupil knows and understands may lead to curricular inertia (Lambert and Biddulph 2015).

This chapter seeks to explore how teachers go about their work, that is, how they make professional judgements about teaching and learning and know what actions to take in relation to individual pupils. Teacher agency will be presented as a complex and interactive process that is more than simply individual judgement and always context-sensitive, shaped as it is by unfolding classroom conditions. The concept of teacher agency is hugely overlooked within the literature on autism and education, with teaching often assumed to be the straightforward delivery of a specified curriculum and 'poor teaching' as the failure to do this. For this reason, the first part of the chapter will not focus on autism specifically, but will look at what research tells us about the pedagogical principles of good teaching more generally and how the purpose of education is understood. Different models of pedagogical practice exist to conceptualise attributes of teaching, including sources of teacher knowledge and teacher orientations within practice. All emphasise the social process that is teaching and the importance of teachers translating specified curriculum into practice, but also building positive relationships with pupils, encouraging participation, engaging with pupils' understandings and extending their thinking. This will be discussed below with reference to the ways in which teachers move between different communicative approaches depending on what is being taught and how pupils engage. It will be noted that teaching concerns, above all, the development of communicative relationships and the adjustment of levels of support in response to experiences of these. Dialogic teaching is currently identified as a set of pedagogical practices to promote open and exploratory talk within classrooms that are most likely to support good progress in pupils, and this will be described in relation to four communicative approaches typically taken by teachers.

Having established what is foundational for effective pedagogical practice, the second part of the chapter will explore its relevance to a discussion of autism. I will present evidence from my own research into inclusive pedagogical practices in mainstream schools in relation to autistic pupils and show how the same principles of good practice apply here too. It will be shown that the mainstream practitioners involved in the research typically took a social constructivist perspective on pedagogy and saw children as agentive and able to bring prior experiences and understandings to learning contexts. Examples of real-life pupil-practitioner learning interactions will be presented as a way of illustrating that, for autistic pupils too, the social process that is teaching and learning is an important one, especially where it occurs within relationships that are positively experienced, respectful and responsive to what pupils know and understand.

Teachers' Professional Knowledge, Temporal Orientation Within Educational Practice, and Dimensions of Pedagogy

Given the complexity of what teachers do when they teach, it is perhaps unsurprising that a range of models have been developed to describe different aspects of pedagogical practice. I am going to explore three models of relevance to a discussion about how teachers make judgements about pupils and achieve agency in their work, focusing firstly on teachers' professional knowledge, secondly on the temporal orientation of teachers within practice, and finally on different dimensions of pedagogical practice that exist for teachers. These aspects of what teachers do will be discussed separately, but it is important to note that each could be seen as aspects of the same phenomenon, that is, the ordinary professional practice of teachers. I should also note that, though an explanation of what teaching is requires a sophisticated and multidimensional analysis, the act of teaching itself is experienced on the ground as quite mundane in nature, involving mostly unremarkable and commonplace encounters with pupils. Teaching is concerned with relationships and, as with human relationships generally, actions taken in classrooms are rooted in ongoing cultural practices and understandings, but are experienced as spontaneous and momentary. Awareness of why an action has been taken may be only partial as teachers go about their work, though may be realised more fully through reflection.

Much has been made in recent years of teachers' professional knowledge and what form it takes within practice. Educational theorists have argued that a focus on teacher competency is misguided since it overlooks the fact that teaching is about process and the appropriate use of knowledge, much more than a matter of skills and accountability (Allan 2011). Teaching is above all a social process and Christopher Winch and colleagues (2015) have outlined three attributes of the professional knowledge of teachers in relation to their engagement with pupils. They identify first of all the situated knowledge of teachers, a highly practical form of knowing which is based on teachers' perceptions of the personal circumstances, interests and abilities of their pupils alongside the specific conditions of the classroom and the availability of resources. Situated knowledge, often referred to as *phronesis* or practical wisdom in educational parlance, is associated with the idea of immediacy and the operation of common sense in the classroom. Teaching concerns ongoing interactions and rapid judgement in the busy environment of the classroom, though common sense as an idea does not describe sufficiently the degree of professional experience and expertise involved on the part of teachers. The practical wisdom of teachers is often experienced by them as intuitive and partly tacit in nature however; teachers do not always know why they have done something and may find it hard to describe their action in words.

Teachers move between knowledge states, often acting intuitively, but also taking a more deliberative and critical stance on their actions at times. Winch and colleagues identify critical reflection—the capacity of teachers to think about and make sense of what they do—as a second attribute of teacher knowledge. The notion of critical reflection in teaching, which is sometimes termed *episteme*, is influenced by the work of Donald Schön (1983) on the reflective practitioner. He described professional practice as involving a cyclical pattern of action, reflection and further action, and argued that reflection is the mechanism by which professionals learn and develop their practice. Lawrence Stenhouse (1975) applied these ideas to education and promoted the idea of systematic enquiry as a critical part of teaching. Given the context-specific nature of pedagogic relationships and importance of teacher judgement, Stenhouse and others have argued for the importance of self-study and the study of teaching practice to the process of translating theory into practice. Action research was and is promoted as one of the most suitable approaches to educational research since it ensures that the link between research and practice is strongly maintained. There continues to be an emphasis put on teachers as researchers of their own practice and of educational research as needing to be highly practice-focused in nature, with professional learning currently identified within many education systems globally as an integral part of being an educational professional. The folklore of teaching is that teachers become stuck in their ways and can be stubbornly resistant to change, but interestingly, recent research by Gert Biesta and colleagues (2017) found that, compared to newly qualified teachers, experienced teachers produce more nuanced explanations of their practice and have deeper and dimensionally more complex understandings of the purpose of education and their role of teacher. Such research indicates that it is important to see teachers as professionals who develop their practice, with experience leading to greater understanding and expertise.

Practical wisdom and critical reflection operate alongside the third attribute of teachers' professional knowledge, technical knowledge or *techne*, which relates to teacher know-how about the curriculum and pedagogy. Technical knowledge is sometimes associated with the idea of 'what works' within education, but, as Winch and colleagues argue, without teachers' practical wisdom and critical reflection, the use of this knowledge alone would mean teaching would fail to take proper account of the social context of learning. The politicization of education in recent years has meant greater emphasis on the need for certainty in terms of learning outcomes and led to the idea of teachers as technicians who deliver what educational technologists have designed. However, as Basil Bernstein (1990) pointed out nearly three decades ago, curriculum teaching in actuality involves the re-contextualisation by teachers of official discourses of education produced by researchers and policymakers in the light of what their pupils bring to learning. Winch and colleagues state that teaching needs to be *textured* and requires all three aspects of knowledge in order to be effective. Teachers must employ intuitive, technical *and* theoretical knowledge within continuous assessments of pupil learning, and this makes teaching practice an interactive and dynamic process, but also a matter for ongoing professional development.

The idea of teachers as curriculum-makers and teaching as layered and adaptive has meant renewed interest in the agency of teachers and what the 'doing' of teaching actually involves. Mark Priestley and colleagues (2015) take an ecological view on teacher agency and argue that it is always shaped by the particular cultural, relational and materials conditions in which teachers work, teachers acting *through* their environment rather than on it. They point out that agency is not something people innately have, but comes about through their interactions with environmental conditions; as they describe it, teachers achieve agency rather than have agency. They propose a model for thinking about teacher agency and the moment-to-moment quality of teachers' professional judgement that is focused on the ways in which teachers temporally orientate themselves within their practice. According to this view, teachers may take an iterative stance, that is, orientate themselves in terms of past patterns of action and historical understandings, or they may take a projective stance, that is, orientate themselves in terms of future goals. An iterative orientation is a backward-looking position that requires a critical analysis of whether and how past experiences are relevant to current conditions. Past decisions and actions may be applied, the teacher required to be able to select appropriately amongst these. It is a position that is also associated with what teachers choose to attend to pedagogically, that is, what they notice and see as of relevance, or 'bracket in' as of current pedagogical concern. By contrast, a projective orientation is forward-looking and will be more closely related to aspirations, imagined outcomes and experimentation. Taking this stance will probably mean attention to the purpose of education, whether taken from institutional goals and the specified curriculum, or aligned with the teacher's own values and beliefs about education. As Priestley and colleagues point out, these two sets of priorities are not

necessarily the same, teachers sometimes creating narratives about practice that show how it is in line with educational standards or, conversely,
re-structuring and resisting official discourses about education. Teacher
resistance to official pedagogic discourse should not be seen as straight-
forwardly subversive however. Educational practice is often colonized by
competing discourses that are incompatible and unable to support a coherent narrative of educational purpose, teachers needing to choose amongst
these to make sense of what they do. The area of autism and education
could be described as highly colonized in this respect. Currently, medicalised discourses of practice compete with a rights agenda that promotes
voice and participation and ideas about education as ethical practice. This
makes it hard for teachers to make sense of their practice in relation to
autistic pupils, something that will be touched on below in outlining
research into the work of mainstream practitioners and discussed in more
depth in Chapters 4 and 5.

Priestley and colleagues call attention to the fact that there is also a here
and now stance that operates in teaching, one that is orientated to the current conditions of the classroom. They term this the practical-evaluative
dimension and see this as inherently communicative in nature. Through
relationships—both those that exist in classrooms, but also the hierarchi-
cal relationships that exist outside of classrooms—and through dialogue,
teachers make judgements about what to teach, with the material conditions of teaching also playing a part in this. Practical evaluations by teachers may influence strongly or weakly what they do, with consideration of
other configurations—such as past experiences or future goals—also playing a role. Each of these temporal orientations—iterative, projective and
practical-evaluative—may be more dominant at any one time, teachers
adjusting their orientation accordingly at any point as prevailing conditions change.

In writing about research methods for pedagogy, Alicia Curtin and
Kathy Hall (2018) describe an experienced dimension of pedagogy that is
also communication-based and flows from teachers' immediate practical
evaluations of the classroom. Curtin and Hall identify three interrelated
dimensions of pedagogy—specified, enacted and experienced—which differ in terms of the configuration of important sociocultural influences and
structures. Specified components of pedagogy focus on what is considered

to be educationally ideal and would include official curricula and societal messages about what is of value in teaching and learning practices. By contrast, enacted pedagogy concerns the ways in which this is interpreted and translated into action by teachers in consideration of relationships, personal judgements, identities and histories of participation. Parallels will be evident here with the idea of teaching as a balancing act that requires movement between different knowledge positions and temporal orientations within practice, as outlined above. In Curtin and Hall's model, pedagogy also exists in the experienced dimension, that is, as immediate perceptions within classrooms, and involves attempts by teachers to apprehend and engage with the subjectivities of others—most notably the pupil—on a turn-by-turn basis. Experienced pedagogy refers to teaching as embodiment, that is, the way in which teachers strive to pay close attention within learning interactions, coordinate themselves to their pupils and in this way maximise shared understanding. Although experienced pedagogy is influenced by teachers' personal belief systems and understandings about their role, as well as the value systems that operate in their settings, it is highly body-based and transient in nature. It concerns the ways in which teachers and pupils are aligned within communication, something that is often tacit and hard to see. Findings from educational research have strongly associated good teaching and support for academic progress with this kind of close relational alignment of teachers and pupils, however, and this has meant increased interest in the socio-relational conditions of teaching and learning interactions, including embodied subjectivities, relational roles and dialogic processes, which is what I shall turn to next.

Dialogic Teaching and Variation in the Communicative Approach of Teachers

The vital importance of communicative relationships in teaching flows from the idea of children and young people as social actors who have prior experiences and bring their own understandings and ways of making sense to learning contexts. Educational dialogue is currently identified as an essential tool that teachers use to engage pupils and understand what

they know, to scaffold learning, co-construct knowledge and help to produce further learning. Robin Alexander (2008) coined the term 'dialogic
teaching' to describe teacher talk and argued that this does not refer to
communication skills, but is more an outlook on professional practice.
Not all teacher talk would be described as dialogic since teachers also use
talk to instruct pupils directly as well as provide explanations, test knowledge and manage pupil behaviour. Teachers often engage in initiation-
response-feedback sequences with pupils, where they seek a set response
from pupils and confirm its correctness, and this would similarly be considered as non-dialogic in nature. Alexander defines dialogic teaching as
a particular set of communicative practices that seek to engage pupils in
discussion and encourage them to display what they know, provide reasons, opinions and ideas, and explore alternative points of view. Dialogic
teaching is associated with teachers asking rather than telling and involves
greater use of open-ended questions, for example, more 'why' questions
and questions that check out pupils' ideas rather than simply acknowledge
whether something is correct. The whole purpose of dialogic teaching is
to engage in talk that is exploratory, expository and transactional in nature
and, in this way, engage pupils and extend their understanding. According to Alexander, taking this approach means the power balance between
teacher and pupil must shift towards relations that are more equitable.
Teachers take more interest in the pupil as a person, show curiosity about
their ideas and seek to provide positive experiences of relationship through
talk. This kind of dialogue and openness within communication is more
likely to support attunement by teachers with pupils' states of knowledge
and understanding, and a shared frame of reference that supports learning.

Dialogic teaching has been strongly associated with good outcomes in
terms of pupil learning and the raising of educational standards. Educational research in this area has investigated teacher-pupil and pupil-pupil
collaborations, but has focused on the processes that produce development in cognition and the various uses of educational dialogue. Inves-
tigatory concern has been less with pupil achievement per se and more
with how this is realised in the relational space of teaching and learning.
Such research has found a positive correlation between higher levels of
pupil participation, teachers' constructive feedback on pupil learning and
pupil achievement (Howe and Abedin 2013). What has been identified

as significant is not simply the use of classroom talk to pupil learning, but the nuanced ways in which this takes place in classrooms.

Research findings illustrate the considerable flexibility with which talk is employed and how it is able to address different pedagogical goals. Neil Mercer and Karen Littleton's work has been influential in this area and they outline four classes of communicative approach used by teachers which differ in terms of interactional modes and levels of authority. Mercer and Littleton (2007) describe teacher communication as moving back and forth on a continuum, from a non-interactive and authoritative approach, where curriculum is simply delivered and teacher talk controls, to more interactively dialogic and non-authoritative approaches, where learning is socially mediated and knowledge co-constructed (see Fig. 3.1). Teachers are able to reduce degrees of freedom for pupils in learning tasks by asking closed questions and channelling discussion towards closure, or they can open up discussion and adopt a more symmetrical communicative position, not stating they know something and valuing what pupils know instead. As Mercer and Littleton argue, what communicative approach a teacher adopts depends on a range of factors including what is to be learned and how pupils respond to this. If a task is too difficult and pupils'

	INTERACTIVE	NON-INTERACTIVE
AUTHORITATIVE	interactive / authoritative	non-interactive / authoritative
DIALOGIC	interactive / dialogic	non-interactive / dialogic

Fig. 3.1   Four classes of communicative approach used in teaching (from Mercer and Littleton 2007)

engagement with it not productive, teachers might offer high-level guidance through directed questions, or they may take an authoritative stance and bring the task to a close. On the other hand, where learning is more open-ended and pupils are fully engaged, teachers may declare an interest in what pupils know about a topic, invite them to say more about what they think or feel, seek pupils' explanations and opinions, and take on their perspectives. Teachers may also say what they think, but offering this as opinion rather than fact and thereby acknowledging the value of what pupils also say.

Talk and dialogue used in different ways allows teachers to support learning flexibly to suit the needs of pupils as well as curriculum goals. Teachers move between directing and correcting, observing and scaffolding, and co-constructing knowledge, this last position seen as particularly important for moving pupils on in their learning. Educational research has associated the cognitive effects of experiences of co-construction of knowledge with transformation rather than appropriation and the development of deeper levels of understanding in the pupil (Littleton and Mercer 2013). Importantly, Alexander's five principles of dialogic teaching outline an attitudinal stance within pedagogy that prioritises the formation of supportive relationships, that is, relationships in which pupils feel themselves free to express their ideas without fear of embarrassment or of getting 'wrong' answers, and where people listen to each other, share ideas and consider other points of view. Cognition and learning are thus conceptualised as attributes of positive relationship, as Rupert Wegerif (2017) has put it, and the effect of being drawn into a relational space where good understanding of the other operates, or is at least a goal. This relational space, moreover, is seen as a democratic one that recognizes pupils as agentive and where pupils feel themselves to be valued and empowered. Teaching that is focused on a pupil's abilities is critical, that is, on what pupils know, understand and can do, and not on what is wrong or lacking in some way. Deficit ideas about child development do not operate within this kind of relational approach to pedagogy since full and open engagement is not possible with what someone is not and does not know.

It might feel at this point that I have strayed a long way from a consideration of autism and education. Dialogic teaching and the alignment of teachers with the mental states of their pupils are aspects of education seldom applied within ideas about support for the learning of autistic pupils. It is possible that the neurodiverse communication of autistic children and young people has been seen to preclude an approach to pedagogy that is communication-based, though overlooked communicative abilities in autistic children and young people, as outlined in Chapter 2, problematizes this assumption. It is also the case that the accomplishment of mental alignment that is a central feature of dialogic teaching could be seen as problematic for autistic pupils, but also for their teachers. Research into teacher attitudes towards working with autistic pupils has shown that teachers lack confidence in this area and feel that recognized ways of working do not necessarily apply (Roberts and Simpson 2016). The issue of mutual understanding is of course an issue here. Teachers and autistic pupils are often attentive to different things in the classroom and teachers may struggle to recognize and understand this fact. But dismissing dialogic teaching as an approach to professional practice in relation to autistic pupils carries a danger with it. As Alexander points out, dialogic teaching is not simply a method, it is an outlook on professional practice. Importantly, it is an outlook that seeks to comprehend ways of making sense for individual pupils and gain a better understanding of their interests and concerns. It is based on principles of openness to what pupils bring to learning contexts and valuing who they are. Dialogic teaching is aligned with educational purpose that seeks to enable children and young people to be free and realise more fully who they are. Transformation in the pupil is not envisaged in relation to a narrow or normative set of competencies, but to a tradition of wider educational goals, such as capability and confidence as a learner, health and well-being as an individual, and informed participation in society (Harðarson 2017).

Dismissing a dialogic approach to pedagogy for autistic pupils carries further danger in that important aspects of teaching as it is understood by educational practitioners is overlooked. This is particularly the case for those working in mainstream contexts who are likely to understand educational purpose as it is aligned with the principles of dialogic teaching. It is very likely that their training and continuing professional development promotes this kind of social constructivist view of education. They will probably not be that familiar with the deficits-based medicalised educational discourse that exists for autistic children and young people. Such a discourse operates more dynamically in specialist settings, where practitioners receive training on autism-related forms of practice that promote specialised pedagogies, but tends to neglect ordinary pedagogical practices typically found in non-specialist settings. Specialist practitioners working in education and health who know about autism and about specialised approaches to autism may actually know very little about general principles of good practice and the purpose of education as it is understood more widely. The idea of teaching as direct instruction often dominates ideas about practice, with the scaffolding of autistic children and young people's learning and, perhaps particularly, the co-construction of knowledge much less prevalent as ideas. This begs the question, therefore, whether non-specialised but recognizably effective pedagogical practices can be considered useful for autistic pupils as they are for all other pupils.

This was a key question for research I carried out with practitioners and pupils in primary mainstream schools in the UK. Research into pedagogical practice for autistic pupils has historically been focused on specialist settings with the assumption made that findings can be generalized to other types of settings. The social constructivist arguments set out here, that posit educational practice as highly context specific and subject to different sets of understandings by teachers and others, would militate against such an approach to research. The aim of the research project was to discover more about the nature of effective pedagogy as it relates to autistic pupils who are thriving in non-specialist settings and findings are presented below.

Dimensions of Inclusive Pedagogy for Autistic Pupils in Mainstream Schools

The project was postdoctoral research that took place over a 24-month period. It was hoped that the aim of the project could be realised by addressing the following three research questions:

1. In what ways do autistic pupils in mainstream classrooms participate in ordinary learning interactions with their teachers and teaching assistants?
2. What teaching strategies are employed within learning interactions by mainstream practitioners working with an autistic pupil?
3. How do mainstream practitioners make sense of their practice in relation to pupils on the autism spectrum?

The study employed a participatory research design in which practitioners and pupils were invited to be co-researchers who contributed to the collection and analysis of data. A participatory design was thought to be important as a way of ensuring the full engagement of mainstream practitioners, who can lack confidence in their practice in relation to autistic pupils and become disengaged with research taking place in their schools (Guldberg et al. 2017). A basic assumption of the project was that the primary research relationship was seen respectfully as that between teacher or teaching assistant and pupil. Practitioners and pupils were regarded as the 'experts' on their practice and authorities on the experiences of teaching and learning that occurred in their classrooms.

Four primary schools in one region of the UK were involved over two stages of data collection. Each of the participating schools had experience of working with a number of autistic pupils over several years, though none had any kind of specialist provision, such as an autism resource base or learning facility. Child participants comprised in total five pupils aged between 6 and 11-years-old, all of whom were considered by their teachers and parents as doing well in school and able to make good progress within the mainstream setting. An important rationale for the study was that investigation was of effective pedagogy and the recruitment process involved verifying that child participants were happy and settled in school and developing in terms of their academic and social learning. Practitioner participants were the teachers and teaching assistants who were working with pupil participants at the time of the study. They were invited to agree a method for recording ordinary learning interactions they engaged in with their autistic pupils and most decided to use iPads, but also a camera system that was already in use in two of the classrooms for teacher reflection. Practitioners and pupils were given a large degree of control over what they chose to record and upload as data for analysis onto a shared online platform. They were provided with advice on how to make recordings in a manner that was ethically sound and in line with guidance from the British Educational Research Association, but could decide themselves what was useful in terms of information. Consequently, some recordings involved in-class learning activity, but some involved out of class activity as well as non-academic conversations between practitioners and pupils that focused on social learning.

Just over 400 minutes of data was recorded over both stages of data collection, comprising a total of 38 interactions with an average length of 18 minutes. These recordings were reviewed and indexed, with both the lesson content and the nature of interaction and support noted. A detailed transcription method, typically used in conversation analysis, was applied to moments of learning interaction between pupils and their teachers or teaching assistants, the bulk of the data comprising the latter (pupil-teaching assistant interactions). Detailed transcription conventions, which record verbal and nonverbal communication and a speaker's orientation within conversation, focus on turn-by-turn sequences and have been found to be useful in research into the interactions of autistic children and adults. As has been discussed in the previous chapter, such research has shown that autistic children have communicative competencies that are often subtle and easily overlooked, but also reveals the ways in which neurotypical communication partners engage. This sort of detail was felt to be important to this study as a way of exploring the agency of both practitioners and pupils within teaching and learning and the social construction of knowledge. My initial interpretations about the transcribed data were checked out with adult participants, and children in some cases, who were shown extracts in follow up discussions in schools, with findings adjusted accordingly. Practitioner participants were also interviewed more formally as a way of gaining insight into how they made sense of their own practice and what they saw as underpinning the good progress of the pupil with whom they worked.

Findings from the research provide a good deal of evidence that pupils were able to participate effectively in teacher-pupil dialogues, for example, by providing preferred responses in conversation and maintaining a structural level of cooperation, with many instances of over-lapping responses and minimal pauses. In this respect, findings reflect previous research into learning interactions of autistic pupils in school settings, carried out by researchers such as Paul Dickerson, Terhi Korkiakangas, John Rae and Penny Stribling. Their research also found that children have competencies in communication and can perform appropriate actions within interactional sequences (see for example Dickerson et al. 2007; Korkiakangas et al. 2012; Stribling et al. 2007). My study was interested in the strategies used by mainstream practitioners within learning interactions and how they made judgements about what actions to take. What is evident from the data set is that practitioners adopted different communicative approaches depending on the nature of the task and what was going on within the relationship. The data set shows that direct instructions tended to be associated more with formal learning tasks that took place within whole group activity in the classroom where stricter rules applied, for example, setting out written work in topic books, or where a problem was to be solved in a particular way. A strong preference existed, however, for dialogic approaches to teaching, where pupils were encouraged to reason, explain their ideas and participate in shared thinking about a topic. Even for children who experienced considerable difficulty in terms of their communication, where outcomes of learning interactions had varying degrees of success, a dialogic approach was employed by practitioners whenever possible. This was the case for one participant, Ben, a 6-year-old boy with autism, and his teaching assistant, Nora. In order to give a sense of the range of communicative approaches evidenced by the data set, sequences of interaction which are taken from conversations between them are presented below.

Nora had been working with Ben for two years prior to the research taking place and knew him well, regularly supporting him with learning activities taking place in the mainstream classroom. From the data, it is clear that Nora enjoyed a positive relationship with Ben and school staff and Ben's parent partly attributed his successful school placement to this fact. The transcripts of Nora's learning interactions with Ben show that she uses communication in different ways: to instruct Ben, but also to engage him in more open-ended conversations that encourage him to express his ideas and beliefs. In Extract 3.1, for example, Nora issues Ben with direct instructions for working on a mathematics estimation problem which involves programming a floor robot. In this part of the transcript,

Nora's utterances are all directive and focused on Ben achieving a pre-given outcome, that of programming the robot to move in the correct way towards a destination.

Extract 3.1 Nora instructs Ben in an estimation task

Nora:	can you place Beebot ((*pointing to spot on mat, Ben reaches for robot))* over here please in this...one of these parking spaces (.) I don't mind which one you choose
Ben:	((*places robot on spot indicated by Nora))*
Nora:	and can you programme him to reach the < playground>
Ben:	(*looks in direction of playground on the mat))*
Nora:	he park where all the <u>play</u> things are
Ben:	((*starts to press buttons on robot))*
Nora:	↑ can you tell me before you programme him ↑ (1.0) what number you're going to press

In this extract, it is evident that Ben must demonstrate his ability to estimate the correct number and direction of moves for the robot, but he is not required to provide any verbal response. He is simply receiving information and then expected to act upon this. This kind of direct instruction, however, makes up only a small proportion of the recorded interactions between Nora and Ben. There is much more evidence of less directive approaches used by Nora, for example, in the form of scaffolded learning, an example of which is provided in Extract 3.2. In this extract, Ben finds that he is unable to build a house out of Lego bricks which does not break apart and we see Nora helping him with this task by asking questions to channel his thinking in a particular direction.

Extract 3.2 Nora supports Ben in building a house out of Lego bricks

Nora:	is this – is this building stable do you think Ben ↓
Ben:	°I think it's – I think it's wobbly°
Nora:	or is it a bit wobbly ↑
Ben:	stable wobbly are opposites
Nora:	they are ↑ that's why I asked you – is the build...is the building stable ↑

(continued)

(continued)

....	
Nora:	there's a different way you could build it to make it more stable (7.0) ((Ben continues to build))
Nora:	what do you think ↓ (2.0)
Ben:	((Ben places Lego brick and structure breaks)) Ah-arghh
Nora:	you see the problem [seems to be
Ben:	[yeah, yep, it's maybe not stable ↓=
Nora:	=maybe not, but how could we – how could you make it stable – have a think now Ben (.) have a think how could you make it more stable ↓ could you alter it in some way ↑

In Extract 3.2, Nora positions Ben as an apprentice in learning. He is guided by her to carry out a task in a recognized way through the use of questioning that scaffolds his thinking. In this extract, the nature of the relationship is a warm and supportive one, but Nora positions herself as having epistemic authority on the subject of building with Lego bricks, asserting herself as someone who knows about this. Nora does not tell Ben what to do, however, but encourages him to think about what he could do. She offers her own ideas, but tentatively as suggestions, avoiding any overt forms of authority and using Ben's own language ('or is it a bit wobbly') on occasion. This is as a way of investing the relationship with a little more in the way of symmetry in terms of power relations and maintaining Ben's engagement with the task. Learning takes place in Ben's consideration of the meaning of stability, which he contrasts with its opposite, but also in the form of Nora's guidance. Following this sequence of interaction, Nora goes on to suggest he focuses his attention on the base of the model in order to build a more solid and stable foundation. In terms of Mercer and Littleton's classes of communicative approach in teaching, Nora's approach in Extract 3.2 could be described as authoritative-interactive, Nora imparting knowledge to Ben, but in a way that is highly responsive to his participation in their exchange. This is in contrast to the non-interactive and authoritative approach she takes in Extract 3.1. In the first extract, Nora assumes authority and Ben accepts this to a large extent, though again, she asserts her right to know respectfully, attentive to the quality of their relationship by issuing instructions in a polite and considerate manner.

Extract 3.3 illustrates a third class of approach used by Nora, a non-authoritative, interactive one that is more equitable in terms of power and supports the co-construction of knowledge. In this extract, Nora asks Ben about his family tree which he has drawn out for a whole class group learning topic. This time, Ben has authority in the conversation, demonstrating his confidence in his communication as someone who knows about his family and can contribute new and important information.

Extract 3.3 Nora asks Ben about his family tree

Ben:	so ((points)) this one is me
Nora:	right oka::y
Ben:	let me tell you something
Nora:	why – why are you at the bottom of your family tree ↓
Ben:	I'm not at the bottom of my family tree – my ↑first cousin↑ is at the bottom [of my family tree
Nora:	[oh right okay
Ben:	as you see there because she was born in two thousand and fourteen
Nora:	when were you born
Ben:	two thousand and eleven
Nora:	oka::y ↓ so why is your cousin at the bottom of the family tree ↓
Ben:	because she was born in the latest time ↑
Nora:	that's right she's the youngest member of your family ↑ isn't she ↑well done ↑

At the beginning of the conversation, Nora did not know that her talk with Ben would lead to a discussion of his age relative to that of his cousin. This topic was stumbled upon accidentally because Nora was focused on Ben's immediate family whilst he was considering his extended family as well. Nora seizes this opportunity for learning, however, aligning her thinking with his and asking him to say more about his cousin. Ben provides a clear explanation of the organization of his extended family, stating that his cousin is the youngest 'because she was born in two thousand and *fourteen*', putting an emphasis on the most important part of this utterance. Although it is clear from her final remark that Nora holds knowledge about Ben's family, what is of note in Extract 3.3 is the way in which she withholds this fact in order to allow Ben to explain it to her. Nora asks several 'why' questions as a way of maintaining the conversation and opening it out. In doing so, she encourages Ben to express his thinking in words and provide reasons for his ideas, which she shows keen interest in and praises him for when he has finished.

From the research data on Ben and Nora, there is considerable evidence that this kind of non-authoritative and dialogic approach is Nora's strongly preferred communicative stance, with almost all transcribed interactions including some dialogic teaching sequences. It could be said of Nora's pedagogical practice that it involves seeking out moments of mental alignment with Ben, even though she is sometimes not successful in doing this. Findings from the data on Nora and Ben are reflected in data gathered from other research participants, which also illustrates practitioners moving across communicative approaches, but showing a preference for approaches used in dialogic teaching. The final extract presented in this chapter, Extract 3.4, is taken from information gathered about the learning interactions of another pupil, Sai, a 10-year-old autistic boy, and his teaching assistant, Alice. Like Ben and Nora, Sai and Alice enjoyed an extremely positive relationship with Sai commenting on several occasions during the research how much he liked Alice. Sai was doing well in school, showing progress in terms of academic learning but also in his ability to participate in all other aspects of school life. He was described by school staff as happy and settled in school and able to participate in whole class learning with Alice's support. Alice typically supported Sai in class, sometimes sitting with him and a small group of pupils who also needed extra instruction and help with their work. This is the situation in Extract 3.4, which concerns the group playing a word bingo game in a literacy lesson. In this single extract, Alice can be seen to move across different communicative approaches to teaching: from straightforward initiation-response-feedback to scaffolding learning and, finally, to the co-construction of knowledge. It is evident, however, that in the final part of the sequence, where Sai co-constructs knowledge with Alice, informal learning is not dictated by immediate curriculum goals but by Sai's own personal agenda.

Extract 3.4 Sai and his peers play rhyming bingo with Alice's support

Alice:	Sai (.) what do you think rhyming (.5) what do you do when you're rhyming
Sai:	rhyming is like (.5) no >you sound the same<
Alice:	what all of the word sounds the same ↑ ((making a shape with two fingers to indicate a small part of a word)) or just beginning ↑ beginning of the word is the same ↑ or the ((hand gestures again 'small part'))
Sai:	er=
Child left:	=end
Alice:	yeh the end (.) is that right ((to Sai))
Sai:	yeh ↓
...	
Sai:	shirt and ski::rt ((looks at Alice))
Alice:	good so you can write that [down
Sai:	[you can have skirts on a car ↑ like skirts ((hand gesture))
Alice:	yes you can (.) you're right ((points at picture)) that's a different kind of skirt that's what you wear ((Sai starts writing again))
Child left:	that's not what you wear
Alice:	you wear a skirt (.) or you wear a ↓shirt↓
Sai:	do I wear a ↓skirt↑ ((looking up from work and at Alice))
Alice:	((talking to another child))
Sai:	do I wear a ↓skirt↓
Alice:	yo:::u ↑
Sai:	yeh ((smiling))
Alice:	you don't wear a skirt do you
Sai:	girls wear it ((smiling))
Alice:	girls wear it ↓ ((laughing))
Sai:	e::ww
Alice:	why's it eww ↑((still smiling and asking in jokey way))

It was evident from the transcribed data and from researcher conversations with Alice and Sai, that the experience of interaction was a more comfortable one than, for example, that experienced by Nora and Ben. Alice was more confident about her support work and described in a more assured way her practice in the classroom. Extract 3.4 illustrates a typical interaction for this pair and provides an example of a conversation moving from talk focused on set learning tasks to more informal talk about topics raised by Sai. Alice commented in her interview that Sai asked lots of questions about the social world and said that she felt it was important to answer these as far as she was able. She thought asking questions was something that was extremely important to Sai and therefore something she needed to respect and take seriously. At the beginning of Extract 3.4, Alice asks the group to define what rhyming is, but it is clear that she has a set answer in mind and reinforces one child's response when they provide this. This part of the extract illustrates an initiation-response-feedback interaction that was first identified by Sinclair and Coulthard as long ago as the 1970s and has since been established as a prevalent and cross-cultural feature of teaching practice (Barbules and Bruce 2001). Alice moves into a different interactional mode, however, when Sai makes the comment, 'you can have skirts on a car', and links the rhyming task to his interest in cars. Sai mentioned cars frequently in his interactions with Alice who, again, saw this as important to him and something she did not want to curtail. Alice adjusts her communicative stance at this point and starts to engage in explanatory talk about different types of skirt as a way of scaffolding the children's learning in this area. By asking the question, 'do I wear a skirt', Sai moves the mode of interaction on once more. Alice's response, 'yo:::u', shows that she understands now that the conversation has moved from a general one about the world to a more specific one about Sai. Sai uses this part of the sequence to enact his identity as a boy within a group of boys (all the children in the group are boys) and show that he knows being a boy is about not being a girl and wearing 'girlie' things. Alice, who in the data usually responds to Sai's jokey comments in a playful and affectionate way, plays along this time too, making a mock inquiry about why girlie things are 'eww'. In doing so, she shows how she is able to adjust her communicative approach quickly and responsively, from an authoritative and knowledgeable stance to one that is more interactive, playful and uses an intersubjective frame of reference. There are many instances in the data of Alice and Sai aligning their point of view through conversation and intersubjectively engaging with one another in this way. No doubt, this is what supported the warm, affectionate and playful relationship they enjoyed, which Sai appreciated so much. It is probably what bolstered Alice's confidence in her own professional competence too. It is what seemed to allow Sai to enact aspects of the social world that interested or concerned him, sometimes asking difficult and painful questions about other people's actions and comments, or acting out difficult types of interaction. But this was always in the secure knowledge that his ongoing positive and helpfully responsive relationship with Alice meant this was done in a safe space.

Taken together, part of the significance of these research findings to a discussion of autism and education is that mainstream practitioners did not rule out a dialogic approach to pedagogy for their autistic pupils. Mainstream practitioners did not see this approach—which is characterized by communicative partners who seek to share a frame of reference within responsive social relationships—as inherently unsuited to the pupils with whom they worked. From its prevalence in the data set, it is clearly a position that was seen as possible by these practitioners and indeed preferred, the valuing of what autistic pupils know and support for the development of positive learning identities clearly evident within the data. There is evidence that this was not something that was always achieved within practitioner-pupil dialogue and that this experience was an ongoing accomplishment on a turn-by-turn basis. In Extract 3.3, for example, it is evident that Nora can align herself with Ben's thinking, but there are many sequences in the data relating to their interactions where this is not the case. In our discussions about the findings of the research, Nora expressed her uncertainty about the effectiveness of her support work with Ben because of these difficult experiences of interaction. She commented that she did not always understand Ben and felt that she, in turn, was not always understood by him. In her explanations of her work, however, an important belief for her was that Ben said and did meaningful things and that she needed to persevere in trying to understand him. This reflected Alice's descriptions of her practice too, as well as those of other practitioner participants. All participants expressed a belief in the importance of the quality of their relationship with the pupil and the need to respect and try to understand what pupils bring to learning.

The view of teaching and learning that operated for practitioner participants in the research could be described as a social constructivist one. Every aspect of teacher agency evident in the data—iterative, projective and practical-evaluative—could be described in this way. There is evidence of practitioners taking a sociocultural orientation that recognised pupils' prior experiences as pedagogically relevant. There is also evidence of the operation of a belief in active learner engagement and the importance of pupil voice within scaffolded experiences of learning as well as the co-construction knowledge. Practical evaluations of here and now responses of pupils crucially supported practitioners in an ongoing way in making decisions about what support was needed. For these practitioners, such an approach to pedagogy meant that pupils were always seen as agentive, that is, rounded as people and possessing dimensionality in their world view. They were not a set of characteristics or behaviours to be addressed, which is a construct that so often dominates discourses of autism and education, and indeed special education more generally. In a social constructivist approach to teaching and learning, diversity amongst pupils is taken as given, not something to seek to eradicate but to respond to in differential ways through the adjustment of practice. At issue is teacher knowledge and understanding alongside pupil knowledge and understanding. For both parties, this is not a fixed state, but dynamic and subject to constant development. Social constructivism theorises formal and informal learning situations as of equal significance and views teachers and other practitioners as needing to continuously engage in professional learning to develop their practice. It is of note from the findings of the research project outlined above that critical reflection on practice, based on reviews of the transcribed data and short clips of video footage, supported practitioners to think about their work. These tools supported Nora, for example, in thinking about her teaching actions, enabling her to see more clearly what Ben experienced as supportive and allowing her to feel increased confidence in her professional judgements.

Importantly, what is inherent in this kind of relational, communicative approach to teaching and learning is the understanding that communication is itself precarious and unpredictable, always vulnerable to failure as Sterponi and Fasulo (2010) have put it. For practitioners working within a social constructivist paradigm, it is not the case that *all* learning interactions will accomplish states of alignment and understanding of the other. This is something that is a goal. The expectation that operates is an ordinary human one: some understanding is possible and efforts made to understand someone, for example, by being open to what they say and do and adjusting one's own understandings in response to this, will help.

It should be remembered that what has been described in the research presented above is good practice in relation to teaching and learning, in school settings where children are thriving and practitioners feel themselves mostly able to provide effective support. It is possible that a critical factor in this is that there are enough good experiences of interaction for pupils and practitioners, with understanding of the other experienced with sufficiency on a turn-by-turn basis. Sadly, it is apparent that in many educational settings practitioners do not feel confident they can support an autistic pupil and many autistic pupils are not happy, settled and thriving. What must be seen as at issue in education as elsewhere in society is the double empathy problem as identified by Damian Milton (2012). This suggests that neurodiverse interactions will, by definition, be experienced as more difficult. Recent research by Catherine Crompton and colleagues (2019) indicates that autistic people and neurotypical people find interaction within diverse groups more awkward and less enjoyable and successful. This, it would seem, raises a question of whether schools need to employ more staff, that is, teachers and teaching assistants, who are themselves autistic and therefore more likely to be able to establish effective communicative relationships with autistic pupils.

It is perhaps hopeful that in current debates about autism and education there is a perceptible shift away from the idea of educational purpose being the delivery of 'what works' towards increased recognition of the importance of the experiences of learning for both pupils and teachers and the contextualized nature of pedagogy. I should stress that the idea of 'what works' still dominates approaches to autism and education and is explored in more detail in the next chapter. However, it is noteworthy that in a one-day seminar about professional training and disability policy and practice that was organized by the SEN Policy Research Forum, the idea of 'expert' knowledge about autism needing to be transmitted more effectively through training to non-expert teachers was strongly critiqued by attendees in follow up discussion groups. Their discussions were also published in the subsequent journal article (Jones 2015) and reveal that attendees saw the idea of a competency framework as problematic in relation to teaching autistic pupils, rejecting the idea of specialisms. Instead, they argued for recognition of teachers' professional standards and the empowerment of teachers, advocating for much more reflection on the educational principles and practices that currently operate in our schools. This ongoing debate about practice and who has ownership of it is what I shall explore next with reference to the storied nature of curricula in relation to autism and education and the different educational aims and principles that exist.

References

Alexander, R. (2008). *Towards dialogic teaching* (4th ed.). Cambridge: Dialogos.
Allan, J. (2011). Responsibly competent: Teaching, ethics and diversity. *Policy Futures in Education, 9*(1), 130–137.
Alvunger, D., Sundberg, D., & Wahlström, N. (2017). Teachers matter—But how? *Journal of Curriculum Studies, 49*(1), 1–6.
Barbules, N. C., & Bruce, B. C. (2001). Theory and research on teaching as dialogue. In V. Richardson (Ed.), *Handbook of research on teaching* (4th ed., pp. 1102–1121). Washington, DC: American Educational Research Association.
Bernstein, B. (1990). *The structuring of pedagogic discourse: Class, codes & control* (Vol. IV). London and New York: Routledge.
Biesta, G. J. J. (2009). Good education in an age of measurement: On the need to reconnect with the question of purpose in education. *Educational Assessment, Evaluation and Accountability, 21*(1), 33–46.
Biesta, G. J. J., Priestley, M., & Robinson, S. (2017). Talking about education: Exploring the significance of teachers' talk for teacher agency. *Journal of Curriculum Studies, 49*(1), 38–54.
Crompton, C. (2019, June). *Neurodiverse interaction: Understanding how autistic people interact with and learn from autistic and neurotypical people.* University of Edinburgh Public Lecture.
Curtin, A., & Hall, K. (2018). Research methods for pedagogy: Seeing the hidden and hard to know. *International Journal of Research and Method in Education, 41*(4), 367–371.
Dickerson, P., Stribling, P., & Rae, J. P. (2007). How children with autistic spectrum disorders design and place tapping in relation to activities in progress. *Gesture, 7*(3), 271–303.

Florian, L. (2017). Teacher education for the changing demographics of schooling: Inclusive education for each and every learner. In L. Florian & N. Pantić (Eds.), *Teacher education for the changing demographics of schooling: Issues for research and practice* (pp. 9–20). Dordrecht: Springer.

Florian, L., & Graham, A. (2014). Can an expanded interpretation of phronesis support teacher professional development for inclusion? *Cambridge Journal of Education, 44*(4), 465–478.

Guldberg, K., Parsons, S., Porayska-Pomsta, K., & Keay-Bright, W. (2017). Challenging the knowledge-transfer orthodoxy: Knowledge co-construction in technology-enhanced learning for children with autism. *British Educational Research Journal, 43*(2), 394–413.

Harðarson, A. (2017). Aims of education: How to resist the temptation of technocratic models. *Journal of Philosophy of Education, 51*(1), 59–72.

Hart, S., & Drummond, M. J. (2013). Learning without limits: Constructing a pedagogy free from determinist beliefs about ability. In L. Florian (Ed.), *The Sage handbook of special education* (pp. 439–458). Los Angeles, London, New Delhi, Singapore, and Washington, DC: Sage.

Howe, C., & Abedin, M. (2013). Classroom dialogue: A systematic review across four decades of research. *Cambridge Journal of Education, 43*(3), 325–356.

Jones, G. (2015). Autism: Enhancing whole school practice and the skills and understanding of the workforce. *Journal of Research in Special Educational Needs, 15*(2), 139–163.

Korkiakangas, T. K., Rae, J. P., & Dickerson, P. (2012). The interactional work of repeated talk between a teacher and a child with autism. *Journal of Interactional Research in Communication Disorders, 3*(1), 1–25.

Lambert, D., & Biddulph, M. (2015). The dialogic space offered by curriculum-making in the process of learning to teach, and the creation of a progressive knowledge-led curriculum. *Asia-Pacific Journal of Teacher Education, 43*(3), 210–224.

Littleton, K., & Mercer, N. (2013). *Interthinking: Putting talk to work.* London and New York: Routledge.

Mercer, N., & Littleton, K. (2007). *Dialogue and the development of children's thinking.* London: Routledge.

Milton, D. E. M. (2012). On the ontological status of autism: The 'double empathy problem'. *Disability and Society, 27*(6), 883–887.

Priestley, M., Biesta, G. J. J., & Robinson, S. (2015). *Teacher agency: An ecological approach.* London and New York: Bloomsbury.

Qvortrup, A., & Qvortrup, L. (2018). Inclusion: Dimensions of inclusion in education. *International Journal of Inclusive Education, 22*(7), 803–817.

Roberts, J., & Simpson, K. (2016). A review of research into stakeholder perspectives on inclusion of students with autism in mainstream schools. *International Journal of Inclusive Education, 20*(10), 1084–1096.

Schön, D. (1983). *The reflective practitioner: How professionals think in action.* New York: Basic Books.

Stenhouse, L. (1975). *An introduction to curriculum research and development.* London: Heinemann Educational.

Sterponi, L., & Fasulo, A. (2010). 'How to go on': Intersubjectivity and progressivity in the communication of a child with autism. *Ethos, 38*(1), 116–142.

Stribling, P., Rae, J. P., & Dickerson, P. (2007). Two forms of spoken repetition in a girl with autism. *International Journal of Language and Communication Disorders, 42*(4), 427–444.

Wegerif, R. (2017). A dialogic theory of teaching thinking. In L. Kerslake & R. Wegerif (Eds.), *The theory of teaching thinking* (pp. 89–104). London and New York: Routledge.

Winch, C., Oancea, A., & Orchard, J. (2015). The contribution of educational research to teachers' professional learning: Philosophical understandings. *Oxford Review of Education, 41*(2), 202–216.

4

The Storied Curriculum: What Is Education For?

Abstract Stories are used by teachers to make sense of the complexity of their practice and produce a coherent account of the everyday realities of classrooms. This chapter explores two storied versions of the curriculum that exist for autistic pupils, one concerning education as a story of recovery from autism, and the second concerning a progressive view of education. Two curriculum models—curriculum as mastery and curriculum as process—are used to illustrate the ways in which progressive ideas about education are essentially incompatible with the use of specialised practices. It is argued that a focus on educational values provides an explanation of why different practices exist for autistic pupils and how mainstream practitioners think differently about their role and responsibilities in relation to this group of pupils.

Keywords Progressive education · Educational values · Mastery · Process · Curriculum

Consideration of the practical and personal in teaching helps us to see the enormous complexity of what goes on in classrooms. In the previous two chapters, I have described the ways in which education involves a continual doing: teachers orientating themselves to their pupils and making decisions about when and how to act, including what to say and how to offer support, and pupils making sense of learning situations and engaging with these based on their interpretations. I hope I have been able to demonstrate that teachers and other educational practitioners make decisions about how to act based on a range of influences, including official ideas about curriculum and pedagogy, but also the current conditions of the classroom as well as their own beliefs about practice and educational values. How teachers see themselves as professionals, that is, what their role is, what they are able to do and what they are accountable for, will be an important determinant of their pedagogical actions. But what teachers see as the purpose of education, that is, what should be taught and what needs to be learned, is also hugely important. People have different ideas about the purpose of education which are based on their personal values and belief systems about pedagogy and the experiences of transactions that take place between teachers and pupils. Personal values in education determine professional priorities and are often what are used by practitioners to reflect on the effectiveness of their practice. Such beliefs are influenced by the training that teachers and other educational professionals receive, but will be experienced as personal beliefs and will perhaps be deeply held.

As a way of bringing together the practical, personal, institutional and political components of teaching, educational research sometimes focuses on teachers telling stories about their professional practice. The story form has been proposed by some educational researchers as the medium most suited to managing the complexity of teaching and learning. In the influential work of Jean Clandinin and Michael Connelly (1992, 1996), for example, it is argued that to enter the world of teaching is to enter a place of story, since stories are used by teachers and other educators to convey the intricate and sometimes competing ways in which official policy, institutional priorities, the social milieu of the classroom and professional identities come together. Stories of practice are used to describe what education is trying to achieve, but also how learning and learners are perceived, what teachers are trying to accomplish and what they see themselves as accountable for. Stories are able to weave together the moral, emotional and aesthetic dimensions of pedagogy (Clandinin 2015). The story form also supports explanations of the curriculum and beliefs about children, the nature of learning and development, and how children should be taught. The curriculum is what translates educational aims and values into a useable form for teachers and must invest in specific ideas about these things in order to achieve coherence. It is possible to examine curriculum stories as a way of discerning educational principles, what ideas and values underpin the content and how educational purpose is envisaged.

Different curricula employ different stories of educational purpose and in this chapter I am going to explore two of relevance to the education of autistic pupils. One curriculum story is that of children as passive learners and teaching as the transmission of knowledge and skills. This is a dominant story that is associated with specialised practices, though it operates less powerfully in non-specialist settings. It is a story that has become slightly more nuanced within recent years, with more allowance given to the complexity of teaching and learning whilst remaining essentially the same story of control of the individual child. A different story, based on different ideas about teaching and learning and the purpose of education, tends to operate in mainstream education. This story describes children as active learners who make sense of learning contexts and act based on these interpretations. Teachers are less powerful as educators and cannot guarantee pre-determined change in the pupil. They must act as guides who support children's developing understanding. Though socialisation is of concern in this educational story, the values that are expressed are ones of personal growth and freedom of the individual rather than control. The writings of Gert Biesta, which examine the value-based nature of education, will be drawn on in order to describe the purpose of education as it tends to be understood within non-specialist settings. What will be outlined is the way in which educational values determine the organisation of teaching and learning and it will be argued that greater attention to competing value systems that operate for autistic pupils allows us to clarify what constitutes a good education.

Autism and Education as a Story of Recovery

Alicia Broderick and Ari Ne'eman (2008) were amongst the first to point
out that descriptions of autism are heavily reliant on the use of metaphor.
They note that terms such as mindblindness, central coherence and exec-
utive function are in fact figures of speech that stand in the place of what
is not fully known or understood about aspects of human functioning.
They and others have argued that autism as a condition is a construction
rather than a scientific fact or observable truth, and that the experience
of being autistic is highly contingent on the cultural understandings that
operate at any one time. Autism as a construction can be either negatively focused or positively focused, but it is the former that has been
most visible within culture and society. Autism is typically constructed in
terms of impairment and what is seen to be diagnostically relevant, and
aligned with biomedical notions of deficit, treatment and progress (Jamie
+ Lion 2018). Melanie Yergeau (2018) describes how people are 'storied into autism' through diagnostic use of neurodevelopmental criteria
that identifies what is autistically relevant about someone, but omits other
aspects of their personhood, such as personality, personal history, sense
of identity, abilities, personal interests and concerns. People are viewed
narrowly—two-dimensionally as some have put it—and only in terms
of their autism. Yergeau notes the circular argument that underpins the
autism-as-deficit narrative, namely that, whatever someone's abilities and
achievements in communication and human interaction, they are never
able to get to the midpoint of what is conceived of as normality because
they are autistic. By virtue of being autistic and thereby located at the
opposite end of the autistic-neurotypical continuum, someone can only
ever be less than neurotypical.

Part of the problem with a deficit narrative of autism is that there is a
lack of recognition of positive autistic identities and ways of being in the
world that are neurodiverse. The dominant deficit narrative of autism is
focused on individual psychology and this also creates the problem that
other differences which might be of relevance, such as somatic differences,
are overlooked in favour of explanations concerned with social deficits and
volitional acts (Donnellan et al. 2013). However, one of the advantages of a
deficit narrative of autism is that it makes biomedical approaches of much

greater relevance than cultural understandings. The key issue becomes someone's difficulty or impairment and how this can be addressed, rather than any analysis of whether they have a difficulty in the first place, or whose difficulty it is. Education is seen as the way forward in terms of addressing someone's identified difficulty or needs, but education that takes a quasi-scientific or technical form. In Chapter 2, I alluded to the techno-rationalist model of education and its alignment with the agenda of evidence-based practice. The techno-rationalist model of education puts forward an overly simplistic view of causality within education, making a straightforward means-ends link between what is taught and what is learned. It focuses on the realisation of pre-determined learning outcomes and appropriates neo-liberalist language about measurement and effectiveness. This constitutes a powerful discourse and puts the emphasis on processes of teaching and learning rather than educational values and the purpose of education. The appeal is an intuitive one since techno-rationalism seems to answer difficult pedagogical questions in a clear-cut and apparently robust way that offers certainty; the agenda is one of finding out what works for pupils and then applying that as faithfully and meticulously as possible, producing an outcome measure along the way to demonstrate effectiveness.

Techno-rationalism as an approach to education has operated—and continues to operate—strongly within the area of special education and within education more widely. The language of education is suffused with technical and managerial terms that present curriculum development as science and professional practice in terms of a causal model. Techno-rationalism exerts a particularly powerful influence on ideas about autism and education which, in large part, continue to be focused on what needs to be done to a pupil in order to bring about individual change. In relation to autism, however, it is evident that the underpinning narrative of what is to be done has been modified in recent years and has taken on a more educationally orientated stance. A shift in focus on interventions used with autistic children—from what is to be done to how is it implemented—has meant the development of a slightly more nuanced view of teaching and learning, what teachers do and the nature of learning. I will argue below that such a modification is at the surface-level only, however, and that the way in which autism is storied within education continues to hold fast to principles of a means-ends approach to learning, maintaining a fundamental aim to control the individual.

An example of the type of narratorial shift I am alluding to can be found in an article written by Connie Kasari and her colleague, Tristram Smith, which is entitled 'Interventions in schools for children with autism spectrum disorder: methods and recommendations' and is published in the journal *Autism*. The work of Connie Kasari has been highly influential in the area of autism and her research into social, emotional and communicative development could be described as moving scholarship on in these areas. However, the article I am going to examine provides a good example of the type of modified story of autism and education that I am talking about, one that appears to present a new theoretical perspective but actually promotes an old one. The article focuses on the use of interventions with autistic pupils in schools and takes as its starting point the fact that, according to the authors, promising interventions produced by researchers exist for use with pupils on the spectrum, but these are often unsuited to the environment of a school classroom and may be poorly implemented by teachers. What is illustrative about this article is its acknowledgement of the complexities inherent in teaching and learning, with recognition given to teachers as decision-makers, classrooms as learning contexts that are specific in nature, and pedagogy as involving processes of what to teach but also how to teach it. Teaching is represented not simply as the straightforward application of research knowledge, but also as a matter of judgement and flexibility depending on the conditions of the classroom and particular requirements of the teacher. Classrooms are described as places where real-world constraints operate, such as resource limitations and competing demands of different interventions. Learning is seen as needing to be meaningful to pupils and their parents, with goals that are significant to children and their families needing to be set by people (e.g. teachers and parents) who know a child well. Researchers are chastised for being unrealistic about the demands of classroom teaching and for adhering to goals focused on 'alleviating the core symptoms of ASD' that may be narrower than teachers' goals in relation to academic learning. The authors broach the subject of the relation of learning to the context in which it takes place, and see the fact that most interventions take place in clinics and laboratories as a problem. They write:

> Context matters for intervention and for measuring outcomes. For example, if the goal is to help the child transition between classes during the school day, then teaching the child away from the school context may be less effective. Similarly, if the focus is on social skills and the child's challenges are mostly in the playground, then the intervention may demonstrate greater gains for children if the treatment takes place on the playground.
>
> (Kasari and Smith 2013: 260)

But this nod to the complexity of teaching, to teacher agency and the situated nature of learning, is in fact only that. Another narrative thread runs through the piece and points to a set of assumptions that are incompatible with this view. The idea of the 'active ingredient' of an intervention, which is a term used throughout the article, is significant. Kasari and Smith note the possibility of identifying the active ingredient of any intervention, which they say must be present in order for the intervention to be effective. This active ingredient is related to the outcomes that are anticipated as a result of the intervention and constitutes what carries the learning and supports the development that takes place. According to the authors, good knowledge and understanding of the active ingredient is what determines effective practice:

> Indeed, it is the knowledge of the active ingredients of any particular intervention that allows implementation to focus on those active ingredients while allowing other aspects of a treatment approach to vary, in order to fit well within a practice setting.
>
> (Kasari and Smith 2013: 263)

In other words, context matters, but only up to a point. Education may concern complexity and require consideration of systems, processes and relationships that are varied and dynamic in nature, but aspects of pedagogy, according to this view, stand outside of this. The concept of an active ingredient is interesting since it appears to allude to some kind of pharmacological basis for education and learning. Examples of possible active ingredients provided by these authors include, pointing or showing an object to share attention, making requests in a given format and involving peers within social skills training programmes. These are characterised as having the potential to work in the way that the active ingredient of a drug works, that is, more or less predictably and outside of the vagaries of social and discursive practices. It does not seem to matter what the quality of the relationship is between the child and the teacher who is doing the pointing or sharing of an object, or whether a child likes or dislikes the peer who is doing the modelling (and whether the peer likes them). Presumably, the power of the active ingredient overrides these things or neutralises them in some way. How learning unfolds during the 'treatment phase' of an intervention—how engaged a child is, how they are making sense of things and what is the nature of their participation—seems to be unimportant. Indeed, though teachers are allowed some element of decision-making in their practice, including resistance to the idea of interventions and unwillingness to change, children are conceptualised as entirely passive. Their role in learning is to acquire skills, which ideally are transmitted to them in the most effective ways. The tone is a resolutely medical one. Interventions are developed by more knowledgeable researchers who establish the effectiveness of an approach and produce manuals of practice to ensure the fidelity of the implementation of an intervention. Teachers and parents require training by researchers and hopefully carry out interventions with 'acceptable implementation variance', though lack of belief in an intervention and subsequent resistance mean this is far from assured. Where this occurs, an intervention can have similar amounts of effectiveness across a wide population and act on different children in the same way in disparate settings.

In Chapter 2, I highlight the folly of overlooking children's agency within learning. As I illustrate in that chapter, how children are disposed to participate in learning contexts and how they are making sense powerfully shape not only what is taught, but also what is learned. There is no fixed point outside of social practices that always remains the same. Relationship, agency, discourse, identity, embodiment and materiality for both pupils and teachers are key aspects of pedagogy that should never be seen as secondary issues. It is these entities that shape the curriculum and pedagogy and constitute the main event, so to speak. Kasari and Smith's take on autism and education is essentially a story of recovery, with change conceived of in ableist terms that assume the naturalness and goodness of a particular kind of body and self. There is an adherence to a normative framework of development, with change viewed as occurring largely at the level of a child's behaviour. The active ingredient works to produce behaviour that could be characterised as neurotypical and curriculum purpose is focused on the reduction of what is seen to be autism.

The point I am trying to make here is that this curriculum story, which has become rather tired in recent years, has been given a new educational twist, whilst remaining at heart the same story. Instances abound of this kind of shift in perspective on autism and education that is really no such thing. Teachers' beliefs about their practices in relation to autistic pupils are increasingly sought, but often judged as insufficient in terms of knowledge and understanding of autism, with expert knowledge continuing to be seen as existing elsewhere. A perceived gap between research into autism and educational practice has given rise to demands for more collaborative working, with collaboration conceived of as teachers understanding better what researchers believe about autistic pupils' needs, though not researchers developing their understanding of educational contexts and the nature of pedagogy. Teachers are being invited to participate in a more equal way in research into autism and education, for example, through the co-construction of knowledge, but then admonished for resisting a medicalised discourse used by researchers that is focused on skills development. More effective ways are sought of translating specialised practices for use in different kinds of settings, often mainstream ones, but with the requirement that these are used in ways that are antithetical to the careful judgement of pupils by teachers, experimentation and responsiveness that is widely thought to characterise good education.

It is notable that within this narrative of autism and education, much of the criticism is reserved for understandings and practices within mainstream or general education contexts. What is missing is any sense that teachers and other professionals in such settings might have ideas about education of their own and do not necessarily share the perspective, discursive practices and curriculum story of autism experts, specialists and researchers. There is no sense that educational practitioners might have different kinds of practices based on values and firmly held beliefs which are rooted in philosophical understandings about human beings and the purpose of education. Inclusion starts with ourselves, as Julie Allan (2008) puts it, and is above all concerned with ethically sound relationships between teachers and pupils. This is an understanding that seems woefully underrepresented within the literature on autism theory and practice, but is what I shall turn to next.

What Is Education For?

The writings of Gert Biesta (2010a, b, 2012, 2013), which critique a techno-rationalist approach to teaching and learning and make the case for value-based education, have attracted much interest in the field of education within recent years. He does not write specifically about inclusive education, but his problematising of the concept of 'what works' is wholly applicable to this area. Biesta notes that teaching is to do with what is variable and requires decisions about possible actions based on the specific balance of factors that exist within a classroom. Basing his arguments on the pragmatic ideas of John Dewey, he claims that the idea of what works will never work because it fails to recognise the socially mediated nature of teaching and learning, the *doing* of the curriculum that I have described in the previous two chapters. As Biesta describes it, education is not a science but a social art that always involves value judgements about what is important for a pupil at any one moment in time. Judgements are made on the basis of relationships and involve a creative process of asking questions about pupils and experimenting with practice. Education as a process therefore is never the repetition of what was in the past, but a focus on future possibilities and what is radically new (Biesta 2012: 19–20).

Biesta (2010a, b) argues that the idea of complexity reduction is an important and difficult issue for educational research. Complexity reduction creates conditions for large-scale and widely generalisable research that is often considered as the gold standard. It involves distortion of the world by identifying significant variables to be researched and gives rise to a 'spectator view' that is useful in the natural sciences. What is needed for the social sciences, however, including educational research, is a transactional view that is able to discern the complexity of naturally occurring and symbolically mediated interactions and actions based on personal sense-making. Biesta writes that, of necessity, good educational research accepts the impossibility of gaining complete knowledge about reality and must reject the idea of trading in certainty. He puts forward the idea that, though schools invest in systems that reduce complexity, such as timetables, ability grouping, curricula and testing, fundamentally they do not exist as organisations in the same way as laboratories or hospitals, where conditions are much more strictly controlled.

Biesta points out that the purpose of education is not control, but freedom. This basic value, he argues, has got lost in debates about what works and educational effectiveness. A focus on educational effectiveness draws attention to immediate outcomes—the behaviour that is being addressed, the knowledge that is being imparted—but takes it away from wider educational aims, or as Biesta puts it, what education is *for*. These 'ultimate aims' are to do with education as moral practice and the values of educators and the wider society. Biesta writes:

> The most important question for educational professionals is therefore not about the effectiveness of their actions but about the potential educational value of what they do, that is, about the educational desirability of the opportunities for learning that follow from their actions…This is why the 'what works' agenda of evidence-based practice is at least insufficient and probably misplaced in the case of education, because judgment in education is not simply about what is possible (a factual judgment) but about what is educationally desirable (a value judgment).
>
> (Biesta 2007: 10)

Within educational philosophy, the purpose of education—the ultimate aim—takes a broad and progressive form, and is often expressed in terms of human flourishing and the idea of living well in a world that is worth living in. Education today has its roots in the character education of ancient Greece, Egypt and India, which emphasised education as the transmission of virtue and the development of individual capacity to do good within society. Later ideas about developmentalism contributed the idea that decision-making and taking action are also key aspects of human development. Thus, the purpose of education is often envisaged in a dual way: as academic learning based on inquiry, but also as social-emotional and ethical growth. Michael Reiss and John White (2013) identify three purposes of education, namely, personal flourishing and the ability to live a life that is personally fulfilling, helping others to lead a flourishing life, and having a broad background in understanding in relation to the natural and social world. Equally, for Biesta (2010b), the purpose of education concerns the gaining of qualification, but also the socialisation of pupils, and what he calls 'subjectification' which refers to the development of the child as a person. Part of the process of pedagogy, he writes, concerns teachers making decisions about which educational purpose is currently to the fore when teaching a pupil, whether academic learning and the acquiring of knowledge, socialisation, or development of the pupil as an individual. He gives the example of subject teaching, which may concern the gaining of knowledge, but may just as well involve support for the development of the pupil as a person, particularly one who is feeling unconfident in their identity as a learner.

Richard Pring (2015), in his influential book on the philosophy of educational research, discusses the purpose of education with reference to a similar set of concepts. He describes education as concerned with the development of conceptual frameworks to organise and understand experience, but also with personal growth. Children participate in learning activities that involve inquiry, dialogue and sense-making, but they also continually engage in interactions designed to support their development as a person. He outlines how education transforms people in small but significant ways and contributes to individual growth that leads to a worthwhile life. Pring further defines education in terms of what is seen as important within society, such as standards in literacy and numeracy, and also in the experience of being taught. He points out that one aspect of school education that distinguishes it from being educated informally by experience (for example, in one's family) is the degree of formality and structure that exists. For Pring, education is above all moral practice that incorporates values to support personal formation in its widest sense:

> In respecting learners as persons (in respecting their integrity and authenticity) one must give them credit…for the personal search for a meaningful and significant life within the range of possibilities. To engage in this search – to be authentic as opposed to taking on board passing fashions – is a

daunting and often painful task…But it is part of the seriousness of living.
And that seriousness is by no means confined to the academically able. Nor
does it depend on intellectual excellence.

(Pring 2015: 30)

In the previous chapter, I describe how educational professionals address
a range of educational purposes by moving between authority positions
in their conversations with pupils. I demonstrate how practitioners sometimes take an authoritative stance on knowledge, but also scaffold the
development of pupils' thinking in less authoritative and more interactive
ways. I illustrate how, in addition, practitioners seek to support the participation of pupils within social relations and culturally recognised ways
of doing things, but also show an interest in their unique qualities and
respect for them as an individual. The extracts provided in Chapter 3,
of autistic pupils interacting with their teaching assistants, show how the
turn-by-turn nature of pedagogy allows different educational purpose to
come into focus at different moments within learning. These extracts convey the subtlety and sensitivity of teaching and learning, how it unfolds
within the pedagogical relationship and how educational purpose is lightly
woven in as enduring values, whether knowledge exchange, socialisation
or supporting personal growth. Though educational aims may be overtly
addressed within pedagogy—acquiring specific items of knowledge, or
thinking overtly about myself as a person or in relation to others, for
example, in personal and social education lessons—these extracts hopefully convey the back and forth dance that is more central to the achievement of purpose within education. No matter what subject is being stud-
ied, opportunities for addressing the broad aims of education may arise.
It is the changing shape of learning contexts based in social practices that
determines the specific aim of learning at any one time. What is also evident in these extracts is the way in which different purposes overlap with
one another and interactively support the ongoing achievement of these
broad educational aims.

Understanding this central tenet of education is, I feel, especially important for those of us working in the area of autism and education, where
pedagogy is often conceptualised in the narrowest possible terms. It is
not that education as it is commonly understood for autistic pupils does

not have broad aims. It does, ones that are usually focused on normative development. These aims tend to be unstated and seen as part of the natural order of things, with a focus instead on what can be explicitly taught. The curriculum as it exists for autistic pupils is typically envisaged only as a prescribed curriculum, but an understanding of education as value-based practice allows us to see that the hidden curriculum is as important. Crucially, the story of education as a path to recovery tends to operate more powerfully for those who specialise in autism than it does for general education practitioners. This is a critical point of difference that underpins much of the tension that exists currently in ideas about autism and education, but remains largely overlooked and under-conceptualised.

Educational Purpose and Different Curriculum Models: Mastery Versus Process

Consideration of educational aims and values brings us to the issue of curriculum. In his seminal writings on educational research and curriculum development, Lawrence Stenhouse (1975) defines the curriculum as what translates educational principles, that is, aims and values, into a form that is useable by practitioners. A curriculum could be described as a set of intentions to guide the transactions that take place between teachers and pupils, these intentions flowing from specific ideas about what needs to be learned and the manner in which this needs to be done. As a consequence, a range of curriculum models exists that communicate different educational aims based on educational values that are diverse. Two important and contrasting models of relevance to the discussion in this chapter are sometimes described as curriculum as mastery and curriculum as process. I will discuss these models next in an effort to elucidate further the values that support dominant ideas about the education of autistic pupils and the possibility of an alternative view.

Writing about the development of a new curriculum for Scotland, Mark Priestley and Walter Humes (2010) outline different models for curriculum planning, including what they term a mastery model which emphasises curriculum as product. They describe this model as based in twentieth century ideas about scientific management and behaviourist psychology that theorise learning as causally brought about through the administration of educational experiences. I have alluded to this view of education already in my discussion of techno-rationalism in education which is set out above. It is a model for curriculum that gave way in the 1970s to progressive ideas about learning as sense-making and a social constructivist perspective on education, but has since been given a new lease of life with the rise of neo-liberalism in the 1980s and 1990s. The problem with a mastery model, as Priestley and Humes and other academics have argued, is that it focuses only on learning that can be measured and is reductionist in nature. Areas of learning that cannot be measured, or are not easily measured, are invariably excluded as outcomes. As Atli Harðarson (2017) points out in writing about the educational aims associated with curricula, the issue is one of closed aims required by a means-ends curriculum eclipsing much more important aims. Broader aims such as understanding, cultural appropriation, personal growth and well-being—what I have identified as the ultimate aims of education—do not have clear endpoints in this sense. They are key features of human functioning and ongoing aspects of development throughout the lifespan. These are aims which are open-ended and hard to measure in any narrow way, but remain absolutely central to the notion of a good education. As Harðarson writes, 'If we only consider aims that can be completed, we tend to focus on the trivial rather than on what is important' (page 67).

A further problem with the idea of curriculum as product is that the content of the curriculum often becomes conflated with learning outcomes. Rather than rich curriculum content developed to produce quality in learning, narrow descriptors of learning become the focus of what pupils are taught. The education of autistic pupils is deeply influenced by this approach to education. Children's communication difficulties, for example, are seen as needing to be addressed through the attainment of skills in communication that are taught as narrow, clearly attainable objectives. Pupils in schools are often expected to master specified behaviours that make up a series of sequential steps. Communication is not conceived of as an open-ended and contingent social process in which who you are communicating with determines to a great extent the nature of your communication. Or as something that sometimes takes a slightly different form. This would make for too nebulous a curriculum under the mastery model and probably be described as 'too woolly'.

Though autism is increasingly described as a transactional issue, this narrow view of education tenaciously persists. Critical theorists such as Damian Milton, Anne McGuire and Sami Timimi have attributed the persistence of this view to the political discourse or 'regime of truth' it supports. Such a view serves to produce particular kinds of subjects within society, ones who can be surveilled and controlled. Control is achieved in education through curricular purpose that sees children as always having something more to learn in terms of their personal development and always, therefore, on a path to improvement and productivity (McGuire 2017). In such a control society, autistic pupils should not be seen as any different to other children who are labelled as having 'special needs'.

By contrast, a second model of curriculum planning described by Priestley and Humes is the developmental model. This emphasises curriculum as process and is aligned with ideas about learning as dialogic, experiential and inquiry-based. The starting point for planning is the learner and what they understand, with what is to be learned seen as needing to be tailored to this. This model calls attention to children's capacity to question and reflect and views the ideal pupil as an active learner who is risk-taking and problem-solving rather than a passive follower of rules. As some educational theorists have pointed out, there are problems associated with this model too. Jill Bourne (2008), for example, makes the point that a process-driven curriculum contributes to the idea of the problem learner or learners who are unable to access learning through dialogue and inquiry. The work of Michael Young (2008), which focuses on the place of knowledge in education, has also highlighted the need to balance experience in learning with what knowledge is important. He argues that a purely experiential, process-driven curriculum will disadvantage those who cannot access 'powerful knowledge' outside of the school context. However, for the purposes of the argument set out here, what is important to understand about education as development and curriculum as process is that this approach rests on a specific set of values. These values are democratic in nature and include respect for the learner, support for individual freedoms and pursuit of a common good. The democratic nature of such an approach rests on the freedom provided to pupils and the equality of pedagogical relationships. For example, respect for the learner and trust in their ability to engage meaningfully in learning, which is a cornerstone of this approach to education, necessitates teachers evaluating their own actions and developing their practice, seeing change as needing to take place for them perhaps as much as for their pupils. This is above all then a *progressive* model of education in terms of the values it promotes. Importantly, it is clearly distinguishable from the idea of curriculum as mastery and techno-rationalism as an approach to education. Progressive ideas are inherent in the way in which teachers view their pupils and the recognition that learners can be different from one another and learn in different ways. The progressive nature of such an educational approach is also evident in the recognition it gives to personal growth and the different forms this may take, with no one template operating for what it means to live a meaningful life. Fundamentally, good education is about freedom of the individual and not about control. Importantly, this curricular story is not only a progressive one of fairness, democracy and trust within relationships, it is also seen to support what has been found to be most useful in terms of pedagogy and the raising of achievement (James and Pollard 2011).

Educational Values as an Explanation for Divergence in Pedagogical Practices

Greater attention to the value-based nature of education and deeper understanding of competing value systems help to re-cast what is at issue for particular groups of learners. It allows us to see, for example, that the issue of teachers failing to implement specialised interventions for pupils may not be a result of lack of understanding or constitute some kind of resistance. Rather, this issue might concern the operation of a different set of beliefs about practice that are not compatible with, for example, a techno-rationalist approach to education. Questions that may be raised for teachers are, not how do I do something to somebody more effectively, but should I be doing this and what am I doing it for? Crucially, the question might be: does what I am being asked to do fit with my beliefs about pedagogy and the purpose of education, about children and how they develop, and about my role as an educational professional? This is perhaps particularly the case for educators working in a mainstream context who are more likely, by virtue of the location of their practice, to have greater access to beliefs about learning as discovery, curriculum as process and good education as concerned with the establishment of relatively equal relationships between teachers and pupils. The values operating here do not support the idea of education as intervention. This idea may be seen as outdated and, importantly, non-progressive. Practitioners working in specialist settings, by contrast, are likely to have been initiated into the idea of curriculum as mastery and learning as a story of recovery. They may feel themselves to be more accountable in this respect, the prospect of a treatment model of education raised by virtue of a child's placement in a specialist setting. They will have more contact with policies, professional learning and the practice of colleagues that promote such a view, though their experiences as educators may lead them to have doubts and questions about this as a narrative of learning. Indeed, non-educational professionals who have good insight into schools as systems, learning as socially mediated and education as ethical practice, such as health professionals who regularly visit mainstream schools, may also increasingly question a techno-rationalist approach and its fundamental purpose in relation to the education of children.

Findings from the research project I reported in the previous chapter, which investigated the nature of pedagogy for autistic pupils who were considered as thriving within mainstream education, provides evidence in support of my arguments on this point. The research was concerned with practice in its most ordinary sense, that is, the actions mainstream educational practitioners took on a day to day basis when supporting pupils on the spectrum. Information was gathered in the form of video recordings made by pupils and practitioners acting as co-researchers and findings show that participating teachers and teaching assistants typically used the same classroom practices with autistic pupils as they did with other pupils. Specifically, they showed a strong preference for a dialogic teaching approach that recognised pupils as active learners and sense-makers, and prioritised positive and encouraging relationships to maximise the accessibility of learning activities.

As part of the process of data collection, practitioners, along with pupil participants, were asked to describe their experiences in the classroom. Practitioners were also questioned about how they made sense of their practice, including what they saw as important in terms of learning support and their beliefs about the progress of the pupil with whom they worked. The information that was gathered provides insight into practitioners' beliefs, therefore, but also the values that underpinned those beliefs. What the research shows is that, though these practitioners appreciated the input of autism specialists, for example, in the form of training courses and visits to special schools, they did not attribute the success of their practice to knowledge gained in this way. Instead, they saw effective pedagogical practice as arising from practice itself, that is, getting to know a pupil and how they operated as a learner, and experiences of engaging continuously in learning interactions with them. These experiences were seen as providing context-specific knowledge that was critical to the success of a child's school placement. Specialist knowledge and specialised practices were seen as something apart in this sense. Careful attention to the ways in which pupils engaged and good quality assessment were described as central features of good practice. The importance of establishing supportive relationships and maintaining a strongly positive regard for pupils and their interests and concerns was something that was mentioned by all practitioner participants in the research. Appreciation of a pupil's abilities, trust that their activity was meaningful, even when that meaning was not immediately discernible, and liking for them as a person were further highlighted as important features of learning relationships. Such positive experiences of relationship were seen as fundamental to pupil progress. According to practitioners, these positive experiences allowed pupils to access learning and participate more fully with learning activities, and it was this participation that was seen to be critical in extending children's thinking and supporting their learning and development. It was these experiences that enabled practitioners to align their thinking with the thinking of their pupils, to understand more about their perspective on learning, and so be able to offer appropriate support and guidance. Practitioners also described needing to reflect on learning interactions that had taken place as a way of gaining a better understanding of pupils as sense-makers. Following reflection, adjustment of their own under-standings and actions, experimentation with different forms of learning support, and creativity in the face of individually distinctive responses by pupils were seen as virtuous aspects of practice.

As you can no doubt see, the values of these mainstream practitioners were clearly based in ideas about education as development and curriculum as process. Pedagogical practice was described in its most progressive sense, as an ethically-based endeavour to support the intellectual development of pupils, but also their personal growth. Interestingly, practitioners did not see development as needing to take a particular form for the autistic children with whom they worked. These children were viewed as mak-ing good and sometimes excellent progress. They were viewed as 'good pupils' who could engage with learning in the way pupils should engage, that is, as active and motivated learners who participated whole-heartedly in subject learning and were compliant with teachers' instructions and expectations. The fact that some pupils needed support to do this, for example, in the form of repeated instruction, verbal instruction presented as visual information, 'hands on' learning activities, more in the way of social explanations, different kinds of spatial arrangements and regular breaks from learning, was seen simply as a matter of good educational practice. An autism-as-deficit narrative did not appear to operate. Pupils were not viewed as needing an educational approach to address areas of impairment. Indeed, for some pupils, who enjoyed very good relationships with their teachers and teaching assistants and who liked to talk to them about their interests, communication and interaction was seen by some practitioners as a strength. Related to this, the individualised learning tar-gets that all the pupils had, which addressed discrete areas of need and focused on narrow learning outcomes, were characterised by some prac-titioners as distinct from the real business of education, namely, access to and active engagement in the ongoing learning activities of the classroom along with experiences of supportive pedagogical relationships.

It should come as no surprise that these are the values that operated for participant practitioners working in schools. Initial teacher training courses, national training courses for teaching assistants and ongoing pro-fessional learning are strongly influenced by such ideas about education. Professional teaching standards, school inspection frameworks and official educational policy often promote these ideas too, particularly in the UK where this research took place. But of course, what I am describing here is *good* educational practice. A key criterion for the recruitment of schools into the project was that the pupil who was the focus of the research was thriving. This would suggest, therefore, the presence of quality teaching and pedagogy that was properly inclusive in the research setting. The conditions I am outlining are optimal ones, where educators do not hold ableist beliefs about how a child should be or see the burden of change as on the child only. Behaviour management, compliance and control were not important issues for these practitioners, probably because pupils were seen as presenting no challenge to authority. The fact that they were considered by school staff and parents as making good progress no doubt gave practitioners confidence in their professionalism and the soundness of their pedagogical judgements.

Clearly it is the case that conditions in schools and classrooms often fall short of this ideal. It is evident that many autistic pupils do not thrive within education in this way and have extremely difficult experiences in school, particularly within the mainstream sector. Educational practitioners may hold different beliefs about children, their learning and development. They may see socialisation as needing to take a particular form and find it hard to respond to diversity. Educational practitioners may be persuaded by the idea of needing to control someone, perhaps especially where a pupil is viewed as non-compliant in their behaviour. This is an important issue for autistic children whose behaviour is often misunderstood by adults and attributed to non-compliant, volitional acts. It cannot be denied that pedagogy concerns socialisation and can be a norming project, as Melanie Yergeau (2018) describes it. However, my argument is that counteracting such negative influences on pedagogy should involve more attention to the progressive values of education and what education is for. It should involve a restatement of the need for trust in pupils as sense-makers, belief in co-agency as the basis of good education, and the professionalism of education practitioners. It should not involve the presentation of an alternative curriculum story, especially one focused on control and perceived as less progressive in nature.

It is evident that teachers who believe in ethical education may not be the only group that resists a narrow, techno-rationalist view of education.

Young people who have experienced this form of education at first-hand can be highly critical of it too. For example, Ido Kedar (2012), a young autistic author and blogger, criticises the didactic teaching methods he was subjected to at school and argues for the importance of a positive attitude by educators, including sharing planning of the curriculum and teachers showing respect for children. In her blog, Emma Hope comments that the best education she has received to date is in a school where teachers have not been trained in autism. She writes, 'They do not believe I cannot do things the other students are able to do' (Hope 2016). These illustrations are provided, not to say that training is bad, but that certain values promoted by some training in autism and education are problematic. Researchers and specialists in autism often call for more training of teachers. Indeed, teachers often ask for this too, but it seems important to point out that teachers and other educational professionals are already trained. The basis of this training, moreover, may be seen by some as more ethically sound than ideas inherent in specialised approaches to autism. Young people's first-hand accounts of their educational experiences point to another way of thinking about curriculum and pedagogy as it exists for autistic pupils and this is what I shall explore finally in the chapter that follows.

References

Allan, J. (2008). *Rethinking inclusive education: The philosophers of difference in practice*. Dordrecht, The Netherlands: Springer.

Biesta, G. J. J. (2007). Why 'what works' won't work: Evidence-based practice and the democratic deficit in educational research. *Educational Theory, 57*(1), 1–22.

Biesta, G. J. J. (2010a). Why 'what works' still won't work: From evidence-based education to value-based education. *Studies in Philosophy and Education, 29*(5), 491–503.

Biesta, G. J. J. (2010b). *Good education in an age of measurement: Ethics, politics and democracy*. London and New York: Routledge.

Biesta, G. J. J. (2012). The future of teacher education: Evidence, competence or wisdom? *Research on Steiner Education, 3*(1), 8–21.

Biesta, G. J. J. (2013). *The beautiful risk of education*. Abingdon, Oxon and New York: Routledge.

Broderick, A. A., & Ne'eman, A. (2008). Autism as metaphor: Narrative and counter-narrative. *International Journal of Inclusive Education, 12*(5–6), 459–476.

Bourne, J. (2008). Official pedagogic discourses and the construction of learners' identities. In N. H. Hornberger (Ed.), *Encyclopedia of language and education*. Boston, MA: Springer.

Clandinin, D. J. (2015). Stories to live by on the professional knowledge landscape. *Waikato Journal of Education, Special 20th Anniversary Collection*, 183–193.

Clandinin, D. J., & Connelly, F. M. (1992). Teacher as curriculum maker. In P. W. Jackson (Ed.), *Handbook of research on curriculum* (pp. 363–401). New York: Macmillan.

Clandinin, D. J., & Connelly, F. M. (1996). Teachers' professional knowledge landscapes: Teacher stories. Stories of teachers. School stories. Stories of schools. *Educational Researcher, 25*(3), 24–30.

Donnellan, A. M., Hill, D. A., & Leary, M. R. (2013). Rethinking autism: Implications of sensory and movement differences for understanding and support. *Frontiers in Integrative Neuroscience, 6*(124), 1–11.

Harðarson, A. (2017). Aims of education: How to resist the temptation of technocratic models. *Journal of Philosophy of Education, 51*(1), 59–72.

Hope, E. (2016, February 9). *Can speech challenged students get an appropriate education?* Emma's Hope Book: Living Being Autistic. Available at: https://emmashopebook.com/2016/02/09/can-speech-challenged-students-get-an-appropriate-education/. Accessed 21 June 2019.

James, M., & Pollard, A. (2011). TLRP's ten principles for effective pedagogy: Rationale, development, evidence, argument and impact. *Research Papers in Education, 26*(3), 275–328.

Jamie + Lion. (2018, April 10). *Spoons and other metaphors: How I use my social care budget.* Available at: https://network.autism.org.uk/knowledge/insight-opinion/how-i-use-my-social-care-budget. Accessed 26 April 2019.

Kasari, C., & Smith, T. (2013). Interventions in schools for children with autism spectrum disorder: Methods and recommendations. *Autism, 17*(3), 254–267.

Kedar, I. (2012). *Ido in Autismland: Climbing out of autism's silent prison*. Washington, DC: Sharon Kedar.

McGuire, A. (2017). De-regulating disorder: On the rise of the spectrum as a neoliberal metric of human value. *Journal of Literacy and Cultural Disability Studies, 11*(4), 403–421.

Priestley, M., & Humes, W. (2010). The development of Scotland's Curriculum for Excellence: Amnesia and déjà vu. *Oxford Review of Education, 36* (3), 345–361.

Pring, R. (2015). *Philosophy of educational research* (3rd ed.). London, Oxford, New York, New Delhi, and Sydney: Bloomsbury.

Reiss, M. J., & White, J. (2013). *An aims-based curriculum: The significance of human flourishing for schools.* London: Institute of Education Press.

Stenhouse, L. (1975). *An introduction to curriculum research and development.* London: Heinemann Educational.

Yergeau, M. (2018). *Authoring autism: On rhetoric and neurological queerness.* Durham and London: Duke University Press.

Young, M. F. D. (2008). *Bringing knowledge back in: From social constructivism to social realism in the sociology of education.* London and New York: Routledge.

5

The Future of Education

Abstract In this chapter, the case is made for inclusive pedagogy as the approach to education that is most relevant to autistic pupils. Inclusive pedagogy assumes that all children are capable as learners and that inclusion requires change in the teacher and her beliefs, attitudes and knowledge, as well as in the context of learning. It is argued that such a view strongly aligns with the perspective of autistic people on education and their prioritisation of teacher understanding and environmental adaptation. Critical issues for education as it relates to autistic pupils are outlined in relation to the role of communication within teaching, the value of continuous experimentation within pedagogy, the need to rethink behaviour management for autistic pupils, and the importance of recognising the professionalism of teachers and existing professional standards.

Keywords Inclusive pedagogy · Communication · Experimentation · Behaviour management

© The Author(s) 2019
C. Conn, *Autism, Pedagogy and Education*,
https://doi.org/10.1007/978-3-030-32560-2_5

Any consideration of inclusive education requires clarity about the relationship between education and therapy. This has been a longstanding one and has taken a variety of forms over the years, decades and even centuries. The ancient Greeks, for example, thought that education as inquiry could be used to treat people who had personal ailments. In modern times, educational therapy is a term that has been used to describe an approach to learning focused on developing the pupil's ability to learn. All pupils are supported by teachers in their capacity to learn, that is, to attend to what is important in learning, to process, organize and recall information, and to express themselves. Educational therapy would have the aim of providing such support in a more focused way for pupils who are identified as experiencing difficulties in these areas. By contrast, therapeutic education could be described as concerned with personal transformation and the development of the self, more than academic learning and the pursuit of knowledge. In the last decade, there has been renewed interest in the idea of therapeutic education, prompted in part by the publication of Kathryn Ecclestone and Dennis Hayes's book *The Dangerous Rise of Therapeutic Education*. In this book, the authors set out to describe how schools have become suffused by a therapeutic ethos that constructs children and young people as 'diminished selves' who should be perceived as emotionally vulnerable. Their argument is that the influence of popular culture along with governmental and commercial sponsorship of the importance of emotional competence to good life outcomes have encouraged the spread of certain kinds of practices in schools. Children and young people are subject to more assessments of their confidence, self-esteem and emotional responses to situations, and there is more encroachment into the curriculum of self-focused activities, such as circle time, nurture groups, mentoring schemes and emotional literacy training. According to Ecclestone and Hayes, the proliferation of such practices has brought about a new sensibility in schools where children and young people are encouraged to focus on themselves and their problems, rather than on the world around them, and to disclose ways in which they are fragile or even damaged. Though good intentions might lie behind the creation of a 'curriculum of the self', the effect is, to use Ecclestone and Hayes's words, 'to abandon the liberating project of education' (Ecclestone and Hayes 2009: xiii).

Ecclestone and Hayes's arguments provide a useful backdrop to thinking about developments in relation to pupils who need extra support for their learning and who may have a label to identify some sort of educational need. The inclusion agenda held out the promise of reducing any perceived differences between learners by re-stating underpinning value principles of education and presenting access to good education as a rights issue. Despite this agenda, labelling has become entrenched within many education systems around the world and continues to be used to define a pupil and determine their ability in a fixed way. As Cate Watson (2010) and others have argued, however, what is a label and who qualifies for one has become much more fluid, with categories of need broadening out and boundaries between categories becoming more blurred. The use of labels has helped to sustain the idea of normativity, whilst remaining somewhat arbitrary and doing little to create clarity. The spread of 'spectral thinking' (McGuire 2017) in the last two decades, which places everyone on a sliding scale between wellness and ill-health, raises the possibility that we all have the potential to acquire needs and blurs boundaries further. The uncertainty of diagnostic definitions and inevitable inexactitude of many treatments and interventions add to the sense that education has become part of the wellness industry, as Anne McGuire describes it. For those of us who have a label, there is the likelihood that we will always be on a path to recovery, though never finally there.

The intrusion of self-improvement and wellness into education can be seen in the development of new curriculum. In the UK, for example, Wales is in the process of developing a new curriculum on the basis of four educational purposes all of which focus on how a child or young person should be rather than what they should know (Donaldson 2015). Critics associate these purposes, which are focused on producing confident, ambitious, enterprising and healthy individuals, with market-driven neo-liberal education policies focused on workforce productivity and successful economic futures (Lemke and Zhu 2018). Such developments, however, make it even harder to tease apart what is education and what is therapeutic education, though it would appear to be ever more important to do so. In this chapter, I present an argument that the future of education for those who need extra support in school, including pupils on the autism spectrum, is in the use of inclusive pedagogies rather than thera-peutic approaches. Inclusive education as it is currently theorised makes the basic assumption that all children are capable as learners and have agency within learning. It does not see what children *are* as providing the content of learning. Inclusive pedagogy concerns a certain professional attitude and openness to children and young people that seeks to define them in rounded rather than narrow ways. It will be argued that such a view of education is aligned with what autistic people describe as good education and prioritise in terms of support. Critical issues that are spe-cific to the educational experiences of autistic pupils are discussed. These include the need for a more nuanced understanding of the role of com-munication and experimentation within pedagogy, and greater awareness of the danger associated with interpreting the behaviour of pupils as chal-lenging and what needs to be addressed. A plea for proper recognition of the professionalism of teachers is finally made and presented as a way of moving on debates about autism and education.

Current Theorising of Inclusive Pedagogy

As I have outlined in the previous chapters, good education is about the personal and about relationships, but it is concerned with a different set of outcomes to therapeutic goals. Education is about learning and learning concerns a self that is engaged in experiences, but this needs to be distin-guished from the idea of self-improvement and a curriculum of the self. Susan Hart and Mary Drummond (2013) have described the capacity to learn as involving the interplay of internal resources, states of mind and external influences. Learning is dependent on key qualities, characteris-tics and skills in the individual, such as the capacity to see connections between things and develop personal meanings, and to be able to ques-tion, reason and explain. These capacities in turn rest on the individual's confidence to engage and their sense of identity as a competent learner, that is, what they are like as a person and how they see themselves. As external influences, teachers seek to help children and young people with their learning, offering support for understanding but also encouragement to participate and consideration for pupils' social-emotional responses to learning. Thus, education is *like* therapy in the way that it is relationship-based and focused on the development of the individual. Good teachers proceed cautiously in respect of their pupils' responses and try to provide positive experiences of learning through the development of warm and supportive relationships. Unconditional positive regard for pupils is the mark of the good teacher as is a firm belief in the ability of the pupil to learn.

From their investigations into the nature of inclusive pedagogy, Hart and Drummond concluded that the same pedagogical principles of effective teaching apply here too. They argue for an approach to education that is free of pre-determined beliefs about a pupil's abilities and identify three important practical principles of pedagogy. The principle of everybody means that practice is orientated towards the whole community of learners with no-one feeling left out. The principle of co-agency ensures diversity in learning is realised since teachers actively seek to align their understanding with that of their pupils and tailor support to meet the specific ways in which each of them learn. The third principle, the principle of trust, concerns teaching as moral practice. Of the teacher participants in their research project, Hart and Drummond write:

> They had an unshakeable conviction that young people are to be trusted
> – trusted to make meaning of what they encounter in school and out of
> it, trusted to find relevance and purpose in relevant and purposeful activ-
> ities…This basic position of trust meant that, when learners chose not to
> engage or appear to be inhibited in their learning, the teachers re-evaluated
> their choices and practices in order to try to understand what might be lim-
> iting their participation and learning. Trust sustained the teachers' belief
> that young people would choose to engage if the conditions were right, and
> so supported their efforts to keep searching for ways to reach out and make
> connections that would free young people to learn more successfully.
>
> (Hart and Drummond 2013: 448)

What Hart and Drummond's practical pedagogical principles help us to understand is that education is not focused on competency and confidence as an outcome of learning. Good teachers do not perceive pupils as incapable and incompetent, or as 'diminished' and lacking in this respect. What the pupil *is* as a person is more an attribute of pedagogy and a determining factor in how learning outcomes are achieved. I do not want to go too far with this argument since, as I pointed out in the previous chapter, the ultimate aims of education include socialisation and growth of the individual, so learning concerns these things as well. But academics and academic learning remain a central focus for teachers. Lessons have content and pedagogical principles ultimately support the teaching of this. One of the dangers for pupils who have a label of special educational need is that they can be prematurely judged as incapable of learning academically and provided with an alternative curriculum that focuses on how they should be as person and not what they know and understand.

This is an important point since inclusive pedagogy is currently framed as ordinary relationships and the teacher's ethical stance on practice, much more than specialised pedagogies. Inclusive education is defined, not as a focus on the deficits of some pupils, but as the creation of contexts for learning that support the participation of all (Black-Hawkins 2017). How teachers perceive pupils and how they make judgements about them are critical to pupil progress and contingent upon a teacher's core values and beliefs about children and their abilities. Important criteria for successful inclusion are that a teacher *believes* they can teach a pupil and are able to make decisions about their education. Recently developed frameworks for inclusion focus on just these issues, namely, the attitudes, beliefs, understandings and assumptions of teachers. In the *Profile of Inclusive Teachers* produced by the European Agency for Development in Special Needs Education (2012), descriptors of inclusive practice prioritise core values and key understandings. It is overtly stated that processes of teaching are essentially the same for all pupils and that specialised techniques and approaches are required only minimally. Instead, teachers' beliefs about equality, inclusivity and fairness are highlighted along with understandings about the relational basis of pedagogy and the importance of respectful and positive experiences of relationships for pupils. Teachers' sense of responsibility towards all their pupils and ability to see all as capable learners are identified as key areas of practice, along with the willingness of teachers to reflect on their practice, examine their own beliefs about pupils and evaluate their decision-making in respect of individual pupils. In a similar vein, the *National Framework for Inclusion for Scotland* (Scottish Teacher Education Committee 2014) highlights the need for teachers to explore their assumptions about pupils. Questions for teachers to consider include, what it means to be human, what it means to be valued and to what extent schools reinforce inequalities and the marginalisation of some groups. Teachers are also asked to consider the ways in which their attitudes towards pupils constitute a barrier to learning and how learning interactions can lead to the formation of positive learner identities.

As with other frameworks for inclusion, these documents give full recognition to the fact that inclusive pedagogy is enacted through the ordinary actions of teachers. Good teachers act in the best interests of their pupils, having a personal sense of responsibility to all the pupils in their charge. They try to make sound judgements about action based on in-depth and continuous assessments of their pupils, which they seek to carry out in an open-minded and fair way. As Lani Florian and her colleagues have pointed out, good teachers have sufficient confidence to take a critical stance on the pedagogical situation and ask fundamental questions about practice:

> Teachers using an inclusive pedagogical approach must hone their capacity to see beyond (or to use Heideggarian terminology 'see through') the existing social norms in their schools to imagine and to extend what is generally available to everyone as opposed to providing for all by making separate individualised responses for some as the taken-for-granted social norms of specialist provision often require. While such teachers would still need to pay attention to the social norms and rules evident in the school environment, the development of their practice would start from a position of dissatisfaction with the status quo. Because such a stance is embodied (dissatisfaction is something that is felt), attending to it initiates an imagining of different possibilities for learners. Consequently, perceiving more as a result of seeing through the taken-for-granted social norms may help teachers extend what is generally available to everyone and provides a 'bridge' to help the teacher reframe pedagogical decision-making.
>
> (Florian and Graham 2014: 471)

It seems to me that, for the area of autism and education, this point could not be more critical. In my many years of going in to schools to provide advice and support, I have found that this is exactly what good teachers do when they provide effective support for an autistic pupil. Teachers ask questions about the pupil's experience of learning and examine their own beliefs and assumptions. They put to one side ordinary expectations and ways of doing things and feel confident to bend rules and make exceptions. They do not deem behaviour that is different is some way as a threat to the achievement of other pupils in their class. As Nick Hodge (2016) has described it, they see a pupil's label of autism as only one small part of getting to know a child or young person. In my experience, it is these practices operating against a backdrop of acceptance of difference within a school that underpin progress in a pupil and ensure the success of a placement. Inclusive educational values are just as relevant to this group of pupils as they are to any other group. These include valuing diversity and seeing difference as a resource, having high expectations and viewing all pupils in terms of heterogeneity rather than homogeneity, working collaboratively and being committed to ongoing professional development (Väyrynen and Paksuniemi 2018).

The term 'inclusion' has itself been put under scrutiny in recent years since it suggests an inherent imbalance of power: that someone must seek to include someone else. The agenda of inclusion is now associated with ideas about equity and social justice as a way of highlighting the need to recognise a common good. A better power balance is brought about through teachers' attentiveness to pupils, openness to what they bring and willingness to question (and adjust) the existing order. There should be no assumption that this is simply natural and good. Inclusion as it is currently conceptualised is thus something that people do to themselves as much as what they do to someone else.

The Views of Autistic Children and Young People About What Constitutes a Good Education

When autistic children and young people are consulted about what supports their learning and helps them to make progress in school, it is interesting to note how far their perspectives reflect ideas about inclusion as outlined above. Beth Saggers (2015), for example, asked a group of adolescents in Australia about their experience of being educated in a large mainstream high school. She found that pupils singled out teachers' personal characteristics as a key determinant of successful inclusion and described effective teachers as good listeners who were fair but flexible in their approach and capable of understanding a pupil's strengths as well as their weaknesses. Good teachers were described as able to develop a strong rapport with pupils, be responsive to their individual needs and show a good sense of humour, as well as provide calm and well-organised learning environments. Jane Williams and Diane Hanke (2007) consulted younger children and found a similar response. They asked children about important features of their ideal school and found that children prioritised environmental conditions, such as the design of the building and classrooms, but also the ethos of the school and the personal qualities of school staff. For the children in their study, a good school was a 'fun' environment where staff are friendly, enjoy being with pupils and know each pupil well. Such findings reflect Clare Sainsbury's appeal to teachers and parents, made nearly two decades ago in her book *Martian in the Playground*. In that book, she famously declared, 'all we need is understanding' (2009: 26) and argued that the single most important relationship for an autistic pupil is probably with their teacher. In her experience, good teachers were people who understood that an autistic pupil is someone who does not need more discipline. Of such teachers, she writes, 'their thoughtfulness made an overwhelming difference to my life' (page 89).

It is notable that for children and young people in these two studies, and for Sainsbury in her book, recommended educational interventions existed mainly in the form of environmental adjustments to reduce the stress created by sensory sensitivities, but also as clear explanations of social phenomena. Interventions designed to bring about fundamental change in an individual were seen as inappropriate in this respect. This is something that Damian Milton (2017) also found in his research into the educational priorities of autistic adults, parents of autistic children and practitioners and academics working in the field. Factor analysis used in this study found that parents prioritised training that equipped children with normative-focused social skills. By contrast, autistic adults tended to give precedence to factors that accepted the individual as they are and took an anti-normalisation position on development. Reducing autistic-type behaviours and addressing perceived deficits were seen as unwise and possibly damaging goals, summed up by one participant as, 'because being normal isn't being happy' (page 172). Milton concludes that these findings highlight certain educational practices as particularly problematic, for example, interpretation of an individual's rational responses to a difficult social environment as challenging behaviour in need of control. The use of pupil interests as reinforcement for appropriate behaviour could equally be seen as problematic in this respect. The goals of social adaptation and normalcy that such practices authorise are described by Milton and others as leading to stress, exhaustion and loss of a healthy sense of self. According to the autistic adults consulted in Hanna Bertilsdotter Rosqvist's (2012) study into school experiences of social skills interventions, for example, these constitute 'meaningless training' that result in trying to be someone else and 'training away your personality'. There is a high cost in terms of the energy needed to be constantly alert and focused on social norms. Meaningful training, on the other hand, encourages the development of positive identities. It supports the individual's ability to manage neurotypical expectations and norms, but only if done strategically and with degrees of adaptation, that is, not too much. In this study, neurotypical people were also seen as needing to adapt their behaviour and modify their expectations. The issue of who should be expected to understand was raised with the distinction made between neurotypicals who know they do not understand and those who are not aware of this or do not make effort to understand.

Expectations about who needs to change in terms of their understanding and behaviour puts me in mind of Melanie Yergeau's (n.d.) arguments in relation to the concept of 'reasonable accommodation'. She argues that the notion of 'reasonable' delineates, in fact, an ableist position on what is considered natural and good. Requests for accommodation are only allowed if they mean that the natural (ableist) order remains fundamentally the same. Yet, as Yergeau points out, it is this natural order of things or status quo that is exactly what calls for radical adjustment. My argument here is that this is what is offered by fully inclusive education as it is currently theorised. I am arguing that teacher-focused practices, such as a sense of responsibility towards all pupils and an ethical stance on practice, an ability to examine one's beliefs about pupils and willingness to align oneself as far as possible with their subjectivities, offer the possibility of radical change. It is these practices that will ensure the non-judgemental approach to education that is called for by autistic communities and that will lead ultimately to happier experiences of school for pupils. As Nicki Martin and Damian Milton (2018) point out, what is critical to good education is viewing the behaviour of pupils as communication about the accessibility of the learning environment rather than a challenge to teacher authority. Valuing neurodiverse ways in which pupils learn and viewing a pupil's interests and concerns and how they attend to things as resources within teaching rather than a problem to surmount is of critical importance here. Seeing the child or young person, not as a problem, but in terms of their strengths and as needing an accessible environment and discrete support strategically applied only when necessary, this is where the future lies for autism and education.

Critical Issues for Value-Based Teaching

I hope that the account of the nature of pedagogy I have set out in this book helps to make better sense of important research findings about autistic children and their experiences as pupils in schools. I hope that a fuller understanding of the concept of situated learning allows us to see the agency of children and how they operate as sense-makers and active players within social contexts. This is something that is powerfully demonstrated in investigations of neurodiverse interaction by researchers such as Laura Sterponi, Terhi Korkiakangas, Brett Heasman and Alex Gillespie. Such research illustrates the ways in which autistic children and young people are competent, socially engaged and actively make sense of situations. Proper recognition of the complexity of teaching and learning allows us to see too why research into educational interventions has so far and will always be unable to arrive at conclusions about 'what works'. I hope my discussion of value-based education and the importance of practitioners' beliefs provides insight into why research finds that teachers may be resistant to adopting certain practices in relation to autistic pupils, though the idea of resistance, I would argue, is an interpretation that is highly problematic. Consideration of value-based education means it is possible to see that specialised practices tend to have ableist aims. These lead to the construction of narratives about the curriculum and the ultimate aims of education that are fundamentally incompatible with progressive principles. I hope my arguments and the presentation of my own research help to make the case that progressive ideas about education—the notion of good education as it is currently conceived and as I have tried to outline it here—are as relevant for autistic pupils as they are for any other pupil.

I believe that a focus on value-based education allows us to see much more precisely what is at issue for autistic pupils in schools and indicates a way forward. Focusing on values, and the tensions that exist between different values, helps to reframe critical issues for autism and education and see what is educationally progressive. In this final section, I am going to highlight four issues in particular, namely, communication and the curriculum, adaptability as a necessary feature of educational approaches to autism, behaviour management and pupil socialisation and, finally, the importance of recognising the professionalism of teachers and other educators.

Communication and the Curriculum

The understanding that teaching and learning is fundamentally based in communicative relationships and that good teachers adjust their communication depending on the needs of their pupils has implications for our perspective on communication and the curriculum. For many autistic pupils, communication is seen *as* the curriculum, that is, constituting what needs to be taught and learned. Many pupils are given individual learning targets focused on the achievement of certain communicative behaviours and some will have this as the main focus of their learning on a daily basis. Consideration of progressive ideas about education, however, raises a question about whether communication should be seen as a major curriculum goal. The arguments outlined in the pages above suggest that it should be seen more as what *mediates* learning and an area that teachers also need to pay attention to and develop. Progressive ideas about education suggest that communication is not so much what is taught, but rather what allows pedagogy to be enacted. This means the communicative acts of both pupils and teachers are significant. I hope the data I have presented in Chapter 3, on naturally-occurring learning interactions between autistic pupils and their teaching assistants, demonstrates how effective pedagogy requires teachers to move between different communication modes, depending on how pupils engage and what is to be learned. Of course, pupils make progress in terms of their communication by virtue of their participation in learning in schools. Language and communication also constitute aspects of the official curriculum explicitly. But good education sees communication as an issue for learning more than a problem of the child or young person. In the event of communication difficulty, progressive practitioners will review their own practices and see any difficulty within a wider learning context, including the resources that are used and the way learning is structured. Strategies typically used to support communication, such as breaking down instructions into smaller steps, visually organising a task and supporting verbal communication with visual information, are focused as much on the communication of teachers as they are on the understanding of pupils. For ordinary teachers, such strategies are viewed as mundane and not as specialised practice. This was something that emerged from my research into pedagogical practices used with autistic pupils who were doing well in school. Mainstream practitioners who participated in this research used all kinds of material, visual, spatial and physical means to support their communication. These were never described as specialised practices, however, or referred to using specialist terms such as structured teaching, work schedules or visual prompts. These mainstream practitioners had their own language for the strategies they regularly employed, describing them in terms such as, making learning concrete, breaking down tasks, providing clearer instructions and giving extra support. These were practices that were seen as ordinarily available and used to improve access to learning for all pupils.

There is one further point I want to make on this issue of communication. Progressive education recognises diversity and sees it as something to be valued. As Lani Florian and Jennifer Spratt (2013) put it, inclusive practice is about accepting that differences are part of the human condition and using this knowledge as a resource for teaching and learning. Thus, progressive education recognises that differences exist in the way people communicate. Though children and young people are socialised in school, the aims of socialisation tend to be along broad lines. It is not generally the case, for example, that everyone is expected to interact with others, form friendships and express themselves in uniform ways. The normalisation agenda that is such a dominant feature of the landscape of autism and education operates much less powerfully within progressive ideas about education, with notions of acceptance, tolerance and individual freedom constituting important underpinning values in relation to the socialisation of pupils.

The Adaptability of Learning Supports

Related to this, a further issue for progressive education is the distinction that needs to be made between different forms of support for pupil learning. Specifically, forms of support that are adaptable within practice need to be distinguished from those that are more fixed as an approach. Educational interventions used with autistic pupils are often listed as TEACCH, PECS, Social Stories, ABA and so on, though, as I pointed out in Chapter 2, they may be used in ways that are quite different to the 'official' version. As practices, however, they are not all the same educationally. Some of these interventions are more prescriptive and less easily incorporated into a common school curriculum. Others are much more flexible and can be used as strategies for learning support in the way this is understood in ordinary classrooms. The principle of structured teaching that underpins the TEACCH system, for example, makes it a highly adaptable practice that can be used to support different educational aims and principles. The system can be used in conjunction with a strictly defined set of descriptors as an alternative curriculum for the purpose of developing certain types of behaviour. Alternatively, it can be used as a visual support system that runs alongside other support systems in inclusive classrooms. Used in this way it can be a seamless part of an overall design for learning that includes, information displayed visually, clear and consistent communication, well-defined beginnings and endings of activities, and other practices that support access to a common curriculum. Progressive education calls for continuous experimentation with practices in response to the particular ways in which pupils engage. Good education involves creativity and the proliferation of practices rather than fixed ways of working. What is probably not helpful is singling out some practices as a fixed 'thing' that requires special nomenclature. Is there really that much of a difference between Social Stories and clear explanations of social phenomena, or between TEACCH and an orderly learning environment?

Behaviour Management and Pupil Socialisation

Perhaps the most critical issue for value-based education in relation to autistic pupils is that of behaviour management. As Anne Donnellan et al. (2013) have pointed out, the socially defined focus on autism as an issue of communication and interaction often leads to the assumption that individual behaviours are socially volitional. For example, an individual's behaviour is often interpreted as deliberate, non-communicative and non-compliant. These authors and others have argued that behaviour may be a result of involuntary somatic differences, that is, a person having difficulty organising and regulating sensation and movement, but that this is often not part of the account of someone's responses to a situation. This makes for a potentially toxic situation in schools. Teaching is essentially about managing a group and pupil behaviour will always be a high priority for teachers. Certain conditions need to be in place in order for pupils to be able to learn. These require a degree of crowd control and teachers may be judged on their ability to do this, but autistic pupils are often perceived as presenting a challenge in this respect. Testimonies of autistic authors in the self-advocacy compendium, *Loud Hands: Autistic People Speaking*, powerfully describe personal experiences of being viewed negatively by educators in terms of certain behaviours. 'Loud hands' is used as a metaphor throughout the book to convey an autistic way of being that requires an intrusive and normalising educational response. Amanda Forest Vivian (2012) in her essay entitled, 'They hate you. Yes, you', describes the angry, frightening and coercive ways in which children were forced to 'act normal' she witnessed in the school where she worked as a support assistant. What she describes is an aspect of education that is an ever-present one for all teachers and pupils, but is perhaps particularly difficult for autistic pupils. According to dominant interpretations of behaviour, the prospect is one of teacher authority and all-important ability to manage the group being threatened by a pupil who is choosing to act in certain ways. As Clare Sainsbury (2009) describes it, autistic pupils may openly question teachers' authority and sometimes assume the role of teacher themselves, but this of course does not go down well in classrooms.

What compounds the problem is the prevalence of educational approaches designed to support autistic pupils that focus on behaviour. These serve to promote the idea that working with an autistic pupil is about needing to control someone's behaviour, and not to understand it as a way of gaining insight into barriers within the learning environment. The emphasis is on controlling and curtailing some behaviours, whilst fostering other, usually normative, behaviour. Such approaches create the further problem that ordinary processes of socialisation in school are seen as less relevant for autistic pupils. These processes tend to be more benign than behavioural approaches to autism and less concerned with a strict template for being. The socialisation of pupils in schools tends to focus on broad aims, such as tolerance, fairness and helpfulness, not dictating rigidly how someone should be as a person. The idea is that personal growth and social competence should be outcomes, but not that people should act in the same way as each other. Discourses of difference and diversity that also operate as influences in schools allow for the possibility of interactions that are neurodiverse and the valuing of these by the school as a community. Compliance with authority can be issue, but the ways in which socialisation takes place in schools is more often through positive relationships and experiences of being valued as a person. This is especially important within progressive education since these kinds of relationships are seen as underpinning effective pedagogy too.

The research data I present in Chapter 3, which shows teaching assistants interacting with the autistic pupils, illustrate processes of socialisation as they ordinarily occur in schools. In both cases provided, the teaching assistant shows a preference for a non-authoritative dialogic approach to communication that seeks to value and encourage the participation of the pupil. It can be seen in these extracts how the role of the educational practitioner is one of relatedness and care as well as academic support. There is evidence of an affective level of cooperation in conversation and, at times, an intersubjective frame of reference on the world. Such an approach requires a degree of equity and openness in relationships. Pupils are taken seriously in terms of their interests and their questions about the world are answered as fully as possible. The learning context allows pupils to enact their ideas and concerns with their teachers and peers in a space that is relatively safer than the real world 'out there'. Extra consideration is given to pupils' individual needs and a moral order based on a certain set of progressive values is evident. Such experiences are a far cry from the notion of social skills training as it exists for many autistic pupils and other pupils viewed as having a social need. By contrast, the focus of a progressive approach to socialisation is on engaging as fully as possible with the pupil *as they are* and helping them to grow. Crucially, it does not require them to change their personality, but allows them to be more fully themselves.

The Professionalism of Teachers and Other Educators

Following on from this, a final area of importance in a progressive approach to education is recognition of the professionalism of teachers. Too often, educational recommendations in relation to autistic pupils overlook the ordinary practice of teachers, teachers own priorities and educational policies generally. The fact that pedagogy is enacted through the continuous interactions that take place between teachers and pupils is also something that is mostly neglected. Good teaching emerges out of the way in which educators respond on a turn-by-turn basis to their pupils. The ongoing nature of these responses mean that teachers cannot be programmed what to do, though professional learning might support them to reflect on some of their assumptions and consider different kinds of actions. Tools to support reflections, such as detailed information about teacher-pupil interactions, will be helpful in supporting these reflections and enable practitioners to see more clearly what is happening within teaching and learning. But it should not be assumed that teachers will simply forget their own practices, beliefs and values and adopt new ones. Rather professional learning should fit in with teachers' professional standards and seek to empower teachers. The confidence of a practitioner in their own professional judgement is important since this allows them to engage with pupils more assuredly and probably more helpfully. The argument that teachers are lacking in terms of knowledge, resistant to specialised practices and unable to meet the needs of autistic pupils does nothing for professional confidence. This will probably not build the capacity of teachers to be attentive to their pupils, open to what they bring and willing to question the status quo, that is, the conditions needed for fully inclusive education. It will not enable teachers to experiment with novel ways of teaching that respect neurodiverse learning styles, something that is crucially important for pupils on the spectrum.

The shift in dominant discourses of autism and education in recent years—from what works to how it is implemented—threatens to replace pupils as the problem with teachers. Indeed, specialised interventions and programmes of support targeted at the level of individual behaviour are starting to be produced for teachers. Strangely, this raises the prospect of things coming full circle in the history of autism: the ignorant and resistant teacher taking the place of the refrigerator mother of old. What is needed is a decisive move away from autism as an issue that requires more control of individual psychology, whether that of a child or of an adult. Overly simplistic ideas about good practice as a pre-existing entity and professional knowledge as a simple matter of transmission of expert knowledge fail to grasp the complexity of teaching. Much more recognition is needed of the fact that teachers' practices are based on individual judgement, but are also connected to wider beliefs, values and understandings about pedagogy and what education is for. More recognition is needed of good education as value-based and concerned with positive experiences of relationships. Good teachers acting in the best interests of their pupils and education as moral practice must become the discourse of education for autistic pupils. In effect, the flow of knowledge and understanding, particularly in relation to value-based education, needs to begin to move in the other direction, with a greater sense that what is needed is the sharing of ideas on a more equal footing. In particular, ideas about effective pedagogy and the principles of progessive education need to be shared by non-specialist educators with specialists in autism. I have argued that it is in ideas about good education as currently conceived for all pupils that a better future for the education of autistic pupils lies.

References

Bertilsdotter Rosqvist, H. (2012). Practice, practice: Notions of adaptation and normality amongst adults with Asperger syndrome. *Disability Studies Quarterly, 32*(2), 1–10.

Black-Hawkins, K. (2017). Understanding inclusive pedagogy: Learning with and from teachers. In V. Plows & B. Whitburn (Eds.), *Inclusive education: Making sense of everyday practice* (pp. 13–30). Rotterdam: Sense Publishers.

Donaldson, G. (2015). *Successful futures: Independent review of curriculum and assessment arrangements in Wales.* Available at: http://gov.wales/docs/dcells/publications/150225-successful-futures-en.pdf. Accessed 18 June 2019.

Donnellan, A. M., Hill, D. A., & Leary, M. R. (2013). Rethinking autism: Implications of sensory and movement differences for understanding and support. *Frontiers in Integrative Neuroscience, 6*(124), 1–11.

Ecclestone, K., & Hayes, D. (2009). *The dangerous rise of therapeutic education.* Abingdon, Oxon and New York: Routledge.

European Agency for Development in Special Needs Education. (2012). *Profile of inclusive teachers.* Odense, Denmark: European Agency for Development in Special Needs Education.

Florian, L., & Graham, A. (2014). Can an expanded interpretation of phronesis support teacher professional development for inclusion? *Cambridge Journal of Education, 44*(4), 465–478.

Florian, L., & Spratt, J. (2013). Enacting inclusion: A framework for interrogating inclusive practice. *European Journal of Special Needs Education, 28*(2), 119–135.

Hart, S., & Drummond, M. J. (2013). Learning without limits: Constructing a pedagogy free from determinist beliefs about ability. In L. Florian (Ed.), *The Sage handbook of special education* (pp. 439–458). Los Angeles, London, New Delhi, Singapore, and Washington, DC: Sage.

Hodge, N. (2016). Schools with labels. In K. Runswick-Cole, R. Mallett, & S. Timimi (Eds.), *Re-thinking autism: Diagnosis, identity and equality* (pp. 185–203). London and Philadelphia: Jessica Kingsley Publishers.

Lemke, M., & Zhu, L. (2018). Successful futures? New economy business logics, child rights, and Welsh educational reform. *Policy Futures in Education, 16* (3), 251–276.

Martin, N., & Milton, D. (2018). Supporting the inclusion of autistic children. In G. Knowles (Ed.), *Supporting inclusive practice and ensuring opportunity is equal for all* (pp. 111–124). Abingdon, Oxon: Routledge.

McGuire, A. (2017). De-regulating disorder: On the rise of the spectrum as a neoliberal metric of human value. *Journal of Literacy and Cultural Disability Studies, 11*(4), 403–421.

Milton, D. E. M. (2017). Educational discourse and the autistic student: A study using Q-sort methodology. In *A mismatch of salience: Explorations of the nature of autism from theory to practice* (pp. 163–179). Hove, East Sussex: Pavilion.

Saggers, B. (2015). Student perceptions: Improving the educational experiences of high school students on the autism spectrum. *Improving Schools, 18*(1), 35–45.

Sainsbury, C. (2009). *Martian in the playground: Understanding the schoolchild with Asperger's syndrome* (Rev. ed.). London, Thousand Oaks, New Delhi, and Singapore: Sage.

Scottish Teacher Education Committee. (2014). *National framework for inclusion* (Revised). Available at: http://www.frameworkforinclusion.org/STEC14%20Report%20Jun(PDF%20V).pdf. Accessed 18 June 2018.

Väyrynen, S., & Paksuniemi, M. (2018). Translating inclusive values into pedagogical actions. *International Journal of Inclusive Education.* https://doi.org/10.1080/13603116.2018.1452989.

Vivian, A. F. (2012). They hate you. Yes, you. In J. Bascom (Ed.), *Loud hands: Autistic people talking* (pp. 183–188). Washington, DC: The Autistic Self Advocacy Network.

Watson, C. (2010). Educational policy in Scotland: Inclusion and the control society. *Discourse: Studies in the Cultural Politics of Education, 31*(1), 93–104.

Williams, J., & Hanke, D. (2007). 'Do you know what sort of school I want?': Optimum features of school provision for pupils with autistic spectrum disorder. *Good Autism Practice, 8*(2), 51–63.

Yergeau, M. (n.d.). *Accommodating.* Available at: http://kairos.technorhetoric.net/18.1/coverweb/yergeau-et-al/pages/reason/accom.html. Accessed 18 June 2019.

Bibliography

Alexander, R. (2008). *Towards dialogic teaching* (4th ed.). Cambridge: Dialogos.

All Party Parliamentary Group on Autism (APPGA). (2017). *Autism and education in England 2017.* London: The National Autistic Society.

Allan, J. (2008). *Rethinking inclusive education: The philosophers of difference in practice.* Dordrecht, The Netherlands: Springer.

Allan, J. (2011). Responsibly competent: Teaching, ethics and diversity. *Policy Futures in Education, 9*(1), 130–137.

Alvunger, D., Sundberg, D., & Wahlström, N. (2017). Teachers matter—But how? *Journal of Curriculum Studies, 49*(1), 1–6.

Barad, K. (2007). *Meeting the universe halfway: Quantum physics and the entanglement of matter and meaning.* Durham and London: Duke.

Barbules, N. C., & Bruce, B. C. (2001). Theory and research on teaching as dialogue. In V. Richardson (Ed.), *Handbook of research on teaching* (4th ed., pp. 1102–1121). Washington, DC: American Educational Research Association.

Bernstein, B. (1990). *The structuring of pedagogic discourse: Class, codes & control* (Vol. IV). London and New York: Routledge.

Bertilsdotter Rosqvist, H. (2012). Practice, practice: Notions of adaptation and normality amongst adults with Asperger syndrome. *Disability Studies Quarterly, 32*(2), 1–10.

Biesta, G. J. J. (2007). Why 'what works' won't work: Evidence-based practice and the democratic deficit in educational research. *Educational Theory, 57*(1), 1–22.

Biesta, G. J. J. (2009). Good education in an age of measurement: On the need to reconnect with the question of purpose in education. *Educational Assessment, Evaluation and Accountability, 21*(1), 33–46.

Biesta, G. J. J. (2010a). Why 'what works' still won't work: From evidence-based education to value-based education. *Studies in Philosophy and Education, 29*(5), 491–503.

Biesta, G. J. J. (2010b). *Good education in an age of measurement: Ethics, politics and democracy.* London and New York: Routledge.

Biesta, G. J. J. (2012). The future of teacher education: Evidence, competence or wisdom? *Research on Steiner Education, 3*(1), 8–21.

Biesta, G. J. J. (2013). *The beautiful risk of education.* Abingdon, Oxon and New York: Routledge.

Biesta, G. J. J., Priestley, M., & Robinson, S. (2017). Talking about education: Exploring the significance of teachers' talk for teacher agency. *Journal of Curriculum Studies, 49*(1), 38–54.

Black-Hawkins, K. (2017). Understanding inclusive pedagogy: Learning with and from teachers. In V. Plows & B. Whitburn (Eds.), *Inclusive education: Making sense of everyday practice* (pp. 13–30). Rotterdam: Sense Publishers.

Bourne, J. (2008). Official pedagogic discourses and the construction of learners' identities. In N. H. Hornberger (Ed.), *Encyclopedia of language and education.* Boston, MA: Springer.

Boyles, D. (2018). From transmission to transaction: John Dewey's imaginative vision of teaching. *Education 3-13, 46*(4), 393–401.

Broderick, A. A., & Ne'eman, A. (2008). Autism as metaphor: Narrative and counter-narrative. *International Journal of Inclusive Education, 12*(5–6), 459–476.

Cappe, E., Bolduc, M., Poirier, N., Popa-Roch, M.-A., & Boujut, E. (2017). Teaching students with autism spectrum disorder across various educational settings: The factors involved in burnout. *Teaching and Teacher Education, 67*(October), 498–508.

Clandinin, D. J., & Connelly, F. M. (1992). Teacher as curriculum maker. In P. W. Jackson (Ed.), *Handbook of research on curriculum* (pp. 363–401). New York: Macmillan.

Clandinin, D. J., & Connelly, F. M. (1996). Teachers' professional knowledge landscapes: Teacher stories. Stories of teachers. School stories. Stories of schools. *Educational Researcher, 25*(3), 24–30.

Crompton, C. (2019, June). *Neurodiverse interaction: Understanding how autistic people interact with and learn from autistic and neurotypical people*. University of Edinburgh Public Lecture.

Curtin, A., & Hall, K. (2018). Research methods for pedagogy: Seeing the hidden and hard to know. *International Journal of Research and Method in Education, 41*(4), 367–371.

Dewey, J. (1916). *Democracy and education: An introduction to the philosophy of education*. New York: Macmillan.

Dewey, J. (1938). *Experience and education*. New York: Kappa Delta Pi.

De Jaegher, H. (2013). Embodiment and sense-making in autism. *Frontiers in Integrative Neuroscience, 7*(15), 1–14.

Dickerson, P., Stribling, P., & Rae, J. P. (2007). How children with autistic spectrum disorders design and place tapping in relation to activities in progress. *Gesture, 7*(3), 271–303.

Donaldson, G. (2015). *Successful futures: Independent review of curriculum and assessment arrangements in Wales*. Available at: http://gov.wales/docs/dcells/publications/150225-successful-futures-en.pdf. Accessed 18 June 2019.

Donnellan, A. M., Hill, D. A., & Leary, M. R. (2013). Rethinking autism: Implications of sensory and movement differences for understanding and support. *Frontiers in Integrative Neuroscience, 6*(124), 1–11.

Ecclestone, K., & Hayes, D. (2009). *The dangerous rise of therapeutic education*. Abingdon, Oxon and New York: Routledge.

Edwards, R. (2012). Translating the prescribed into the enacted curriculum in college and school. In T. Fenwick & R. Edwards (Eds.), *Researching education through actor-network theory* (pp. 23–39). Chichester, West Sussex: Wiley-Blackwell.

Edwards, R., & Fenwick, T. (2015). Critique and politics: A sociomaterialist intervention. *Educational Philosophy and Theory, 47*(13–14), 1385–1404.

European Agency for Development in Special Needs Education. (2012). *Profile of inclusive teachers*. Odense, Denmark: European Agency for Development in Special Needs Education.

Fenwick, T., Edwards, R., & Sawchuk, P. (2011). *Emerging approaches to educational research: Tracing the socio-material*. Abingdon, Oxon and New York: Routledge.

Finch, K., Watson, R., & MacGregor, C. (2013). Teacher needs for educating children with autism spectrum disorders in the general education classroom. *Journal of Special Education Apprenticeship, 2*(2), 1–26.

Florian, L. (2017). Teacher education for the changing demographics of schooling: Inclusive education for each and every learner. In L. Florian &

N. Pantić (Eds.), *Teacher education for the changing demographics of schooling: Issues for research and practice* (pp. 9–20). Dordrecht: Springer.

Florian, L., & Graham, A. (2014). Can an expanded interpretation of phronesis support teacher professional development for inclusion? *Cambridge Journal of Education, 44*(4), 465–478.

Florian, L., & Spratt, J. (2013). Enacting inclusion: A framework for interrogating inclusive practice. *European Journal of Special Needs Education, 28*(2), 119–135.

Gee, J. (2008). A sociocultural perspective on opportunity to learn. In P. A. Moss, D. C. Pullin, J. P. Gee, E. H. Haertel, & L. J. Young (Eds.), *Assessment, equity, and opportunity to learn* (pp. 76–108). Cambridge, New York, Melbourne, Madrid, Cape Town, Singapore, São Paulo, and New Delhi: Cambridge University Press.

Geils, C., & Knoetze, J. (2008). Conversations with Barney: A conversation analysis of interactions with a child with autism. *South African Journal of Psychology, 38*(1), 200–224.

Goodley, D., Lawthom, R., & Runswick-Cole, K. (2014). Posthuman disability studies. *Subjectivity, 7*(4), 342–361.

Guldberg, K., Parsons, S., Porayska-Pomsta, K., & Keay-Bright, W. (2017). Challenging the knowledge-transfer orthodoxy: Knowledge co-construction in technology-enhanced learning for children with autism. *British Educational Research Journal, 43*(2), 394–413.

Hadcroft, W. (2005). *The feeling's unmutual: Growing up with Asperger syndrome (undiagnosed)*. London and Philadelphia: Jessica Kingsley Publishers.

Hammersley, M. (2005). Is the evidence-based practice movement doing more good than harm? Reflections on Iain Chalmers' case for research-based policy making and practice. *Evidence and Policy: A Journal of Research, Debate and Practice, 1*(1), 85–100.

Harðarson, A. (2017). Aims of education: How to resist the temptation of technocratic models. *Journal of Philosophy of Education, 51*(1), 59–72.

Hart, S., & Drummond, M. J. (2013). Learning without limits: Constructing a pedagogy free from determinist beliefs about ability. In L. Florian (Ed.), *The Sage handbook of special education* (pp. 439–458). Los Angeles, London, New Delhi, Singapore, and Washington, DC: Sage.

Heasman, B., & Gillespie, A. (2018). Neurodivergent intersubjectivity: Distinctive features of how autistic people create shared understanding. *Autism, 23*(4), 910–921.

Higashida, N. (2013). *The reason I jump: One boy's voice from the silence of autism* (K. A. Yoshida & D. Mitchell, Trans.). London: Sceptre.

Hodge, N. (2016). Schools with labels. In K. Runswick-Cole, R. Mallett, & S. Timimi (Eds.), *Re-thinking autism: Diagnosis, identity and equality* (pp. 185–203). London and Philadelphia: Jessica Kingsley Publishers.

Hope, E. (2016, February 9). *Can speech challenged students get an appropriate education?* Emma's Hope Book: Living Being Autistic. Available at: https://emmashopebook.com/2016/02/09/can-speech-challenged-students-get-an-appropriate-education/. Accessed 21 June 2019.

Howe, C., & Abedin, M. (2013). Classroom dialogue: A systematic review across four decades of research. *Cambridge Journal of Education, 43*(3), 325–356.

Humphrey, N., & Hebron, J. (2015). Bullying of children and adolescents with autism spectrum conditions: A 'state of the field' review. *International Journal of Inclusive Education, 19*(8), 845–862.

James, M., & Pollard, A. (2011). TLRP's ten principles for effective pedagogy: Rationale, development, evidence, argument and impact. *Research Papers in Education, 26*(3), 275–328.

Jamie + Lion (2018, April 10). *Spoons and other metaphors: How I use my social care budget.* Available at: https://network.autism.org.uk/knowledge/insight-opinion/how-i-use-my-social-care-budget. Accessed 26 April 2019.

Jones, G. (2015). Autism: Enhancing whole school practice and the skills and understanding of the workforce. *Journal of Research in Special Educational Needs, 15*(2), 139–163.

Jordan, R., & Powell, S. (1996). Therapist drift: Identifying a new phenomenon in evaluating therapeutic approaches. In G. Linfoot & P. Shattock (Eds.), *Therapeutic intervention in autism* (pp. 21–30). Sunderland: Autism Research Centre, University of Sutherland.

Karmiloff-Smith, A. (2009). Nativism versus neuroconstructivism: Rethinking the study of developmental disorders. *Developmental Psychology, 45*(1), 56–63.

Kasari, C., & Smith, T. (2013). Interventions in schools for children with autism spectrum disorder: Methods and recommendations. *Autism, 17*(3), 254–667.

Kedar, I. (2012). *Ido in Autismland: Climbing out of autism's silent prison.* Sharon Kedar.

Keen, D., Webster, A., & Ridley, G. (2016). How well are children with autism spectrum disorder doing academically at school? An overview of the literature. *Autism, 20*(3), 276–294.

Korkiakangas, T. K. (2018). *Communication, gaze and autism: A multimodal interaction perspective.* London and New York: Routledge.

Korkiakangas, T. K., Rae, J. P., & Dickerson, P. (2012). The interactional work of repeated talk between a teacher and a child with autism. *Journal of Interactional Research in Communication Disorders, 3*(1), 1–25.

Lambert, D., & Biddulph, M. (2015). The dialogic space offered by curriculum-making in the process of learning to teach, and the creation of a progressive knowledge-led curriculum. *Asia-Pacific Journal of Teacher Education, 43*(3), 210–224.

Lawson, W. (2011). *The passionate mind: How pupil with autism learn.* London and Philadelphia: Jessica Kingsley Publishers.

Lemke, M., & Zhu, L. (2018). Successful futures? New economy business logics, child rights, and Welsh educational reform. *Policy Futures in Education, 16*(3), 251–276.

Lenz Taguchi, H. (2011). Investigating learning, participation and becoming in early childhood practices with a relational materialist approach. *Global Studies of Childhood, 1*(1), 36–50.

Levy, A., & Perry, A. (2011). Outcomes in adolescents and adults with autism: A review of the literature. *Research in Autism Spectrum Disorders, 5*(4), 1271–1282.

Littleton, K., & Mercer, N. (2013). *Interthinking: Putting talk to work.* London and New York: Routledge.

Martin, N., & Milton, D. (2018). Supporting the inclusion of autistic children. In G. Knowles (Ed.), *Supporting inclusive practice and ensuring opportunity is equal for all* (pp. 111–124). Abingdon, Oxon: Routledge.

McGregor, C. (2014). From social movement learning to sociomaterial movement learning? Addressing the possibilities and limits of new materialism. *Studies in the Education of Adults, 48*(2), 211–227.

McGuire, A. (2017). De-regulating disorder: On the rise of the spectrum as a neoliberal metric of human value. *Journal of Literacy and Cultural Disability Studies, 11*(4), 403–421.

Mercer, N. (2000). *Words and minds: How we use language to think together.* London: Routledge.

Mercer, N., & Littleton, K. (2007). *Dialogue and the development of children's thinking.* London: Routledge.

Milton, D. E. M. (2012). On the ontological status of autism: The 'double empathy problem'. *Disability and Society, 27*(6), 883–887.

Milton, D. E. M. (2014). So what exactly are autism interventions intervening with? *Good Autism Practice, 15*(2), 6–14.

Milton, D. E. M. (2017). Educational discourse and the autistic student: A study using Q-sort methodology. In *A mismatch of salience: Explorations of the nature of autism from theory to practice* (pp. 163–179). Hove, East Sussex: Pavilion.

Molloy, H., & Vasil, L. (2002). The social construction of Asperger syndrome: The pathologising of difference? *Disability and Society, 17*(6), 659–669.

Mukhopadhyay, T. R. (2008). *How can I talk if my lips don't move?* New York: Arcade Publishing.

Murray, D., Lesser, M., & Lawson, W. (2005). Attention, monotropism and the diagnostic criteria for autism. *Autism, 9*(2), 139–156.

Parliament. House of Commons. (2016, April 21). *Autism—Overview of UK policy and services* (Briefing Paper CBP 07172). London: House of Commons Library. Available at: https://researchbriefings.parliament.uk/ResearchBriefing/Summary/CBP-7172. Accessed 2 November 2018.

Priestley, M., Biesta, G. J. J., & Robinson, S. (2015). *Teacher agency: An ecological approach.* London and New York: Bloomsbury.

Priestley, M., & Humes, W. (2010). The development of Scotland's Curriculum for Excellence: Amnesia and déjà vu. *Oxford Review of Education, 36*(3), 345–361.

Pring, R. (2015). *Philosophy of educational research* (3rd ed.). London, Oxford, New York, New Delhi, and Sydney: Bloomsbury.

Prizant, B. (1983). Language acquisition and communicative behavior in autism: Toward an understanding of the 'whole' of it. *Journal of Speech and Hearing Disorders, 48*(3), 296–307.

Qvortrup, A., & Qvortrup, L. (2018). Inclusion: Dimensions of inclusion in education. *International Journal of Inclusive Education, 22*(7), 803–817.

Reiss, M. J., & White, J. (2013). *An aims-based curriculum: The significance of human flourishing for schools.* London: Institute of Education Press.

Roberts, J., & Simpson, K. (2016). A review of research into stakeholder perspectives on inclusion of students with autism in mainstream schools. *International Journal of Inclusive Education, 20*(10), 1084–1096.

Sacks, H., Schegloff, E., & Jefferson, G. (1974). A simplest systematics for the organisation of turn-taking for conversation. *Language, 50*(4), 696–735.

Saggers, B. (2015). Student perceptions: Improving the educational experiences of high school students on the autism spectrum. *Improving Schools, 18*(1), 35–45.

Sainsbury, C. (2009). *Martian in the playground: Understanding the schoolchild with Asperger's syndrome* (Rev. ed.). London, Thousand Oaks, New Delhi, and Singapore: Sage.

Schön, D. (1983). *The reflective practitioner: How professionals think in action.* New York: Basic Books.

Scottish Teacher Education Committee. (2014). *National framework for inclusion* (Revised). Available at: http://www.frameworkforinclusion.org/STEC14%20Report%20Jun(PDF%20V).pdf. Accessed 18 June 2018.

Silberman, S. (2012). Autism awareness is not enough: Here's how to change the world. In J. Bascom (Ed.), *Loud hands: Autistic people talking* (pp. 358–390). Washington, DC: The Autistic Self Advocacy Network.

Sinclair, J. (1993). Don't mourn for us. *Our voice*, Autism Network International Newsletter, 1 (3). Available at: https://www.autreat.com/dont_mourn.html. Accessed 1 November 2018.

Sinclair, J. (2013). Why I dislike "person first" language. *Autonomy, the Critical Journal of Interdisciplinary Autism Studies, 1*(2). Available at: http://www.larry-arnold.net/Autonomy/index.php/autonomy/article/view/OP1/pdf. Accessed 1 November 2018.

Solomon, O. (2015). 'But he'll fall!': Children with autism, interspecies intersubjectivity, and the problem of 'being social'. *Culture, Medicine and Psychiatry, 39*(2), 323–344.

Stenhouse, L. (1975). *An introduction to curriculum research and development.* London: Heinemann Educational.

Sterponi, L., & Fasulo, A. (2010). 'How to go on': Intersubjectivity and progressivity in the communication of a child with autism. *Ethos, 38*(1), 116–142.

Sterponi, L., & Shankey, J. (2014). Rethinking echolalia: Repetition as interactional resource in the communication of a child with autism. *Journal of Child Language, 41*(2), 275–304.

Stribling, P., Rae, J. P., & Dickerson, P. (2007). Two forms of spoken repetition in a girl with autism. *International Journal of Language and Communication Disorders, 42*(4), 427–444.

Thomas, G. (2013). A review of thinking and research about inclusive education policy, with suggestions for a new kind of inclusive thinking. *British Educational Research Journal, 39*(3), 473–490.

Timimi, S., & McCabe, B. (2016). What have we learned from the science of autism? In K. Runswick-Cole, R. Mallett, & S. Timimi (Eds.), *Re-thinking autism: Diagnosis, identity and equality* (pp. 30–48). London and Philadelphia: Jessica Kingsley Publishers.

Unstrange Mind. (2016, October 7). *Autistic inertia: An overview.* Available at: http://unstrangemind.com/autistic-inertia-an-overview/. Accessed 24 April 2019.

Väyrynen, S., & Paksuniemi, M. (2018). Translating inclusive values into pedagogical actions. *International Journal of Inclusive Education.* https://doi.org/10.1080/13603116.2018.1452989.

Vivian, A. F. (2012). They hate you. Yes, you. In J. Bascom (Ed.), *Loud hands: Autistic people talking* (pp. 183–188). Washington, DC: The Autistic Self Advocacy Network.

Watson, C. (2010). Educational policy in Scotland: Inclusion and the control society. *Discourse: Studies in the Cultural Politics of Education, 31*(1), 93–104.

Wegerif, R. (2017). A dialogic theory of teaching thinking. In L. Kerslake & R. Wegerif (Eds.), *The theory of teaching thinking* (pp. 89–104). London and New York: Routledge.

Williams, J., & Hanke, D. (2007). 'Do you know what sort of school I want?': Optimum features of school provision for pupils with autistic spectrum disorder. *Good Autism Practice, 8*(2), 51–63.

Winch, C., Oancea, A., & Orchard, J. (2015). The contribution of educational research to teachers' professional learning: Philosophical understandings. *Oxford Review of Education, 41*(2), 202–216.

Wong, C., Odom, S. L., Hume, K. A., Cox, A. W., Fettig, A., Kucharczyk, S., et al. (2015). Evidence-based practices for children, youth, and young adults with autism spectrum disorder: A comprehensive review. *Journal of Autism and Developmental Disorders, 45*(7), 1951–1966.

Yergeau, M. (2018). *Authoring autism: On rhetoric and neurological queerness.* Durham and London: Duke University Press.

Yergeau, M. (n.d.). *Accommodating.* Available at: http://kairos.technorhetoric. net/18.1/coverweb/yergeau-et-al/pages/reason/accom.html. Accessed 18 June 2019.

Young, M. F. D. (2008). *Bringing knowledge back in: From social constructivism to social realism in the sociology of education.* London and New York: Routledge.

Index

CPI Antony Rowe
Eastbourne, UK
May 05, 2020